# LONDON WAR MEMORIALS

## A photographic portrayal

Barbara Glebska

LONDON WAR MEMORIALS
A photographic portrayal

First Edition 2018

Copyright©2018 Barbara Glebska
Photographs Copyright©2018 Barbara Glebska
www.harrowphotographer.co.uk
www.barbara-glebska.co.uk

Main text: Copyright©Historic England 2018
The National Heritage List Text Entries contained in this material were obtained in 2018.
The most publicly available up to date National Heritage List Text Entries can be obtained from
http://www.historicengland.org.uk/listing/the-list/

All rights reserved.
No part of this publication may be reproduced, stored in a retrieval system or transmitted, in any form or by any means, electronic, mechanical, photocopying, recording or otherwise, without the prior written permission of the copyright holder.

ISBN-13: 978-1-5272-3450-5

# CONTENTS

INTRODUCTION  5
Map  7

**London E1**
Civilian Deaths of East London  9
**London E2**
Stairway to Heaven  10
**London E3**
Gas Workers Memorial  11
**London E4**
Chingford War Memorial  12
**London E6**
East Ham War Memorial  13
**London E8**
St John at Hackney War Memorial  14
**London E14**
Children of Upper North Street School  15
**London E17**
Walthamstow War Memorial  16
**London EC1**
Postal Workers War Memorial  17
Prudential War Memorial  18
Royal Fusiliers War Memorial  19
**London EC2**
Great Eastern Railway War Memorial  20
Kindertransport Sculpture  21
**London EC3**
City and County of London Troops  22
Falklands Merchant Seafarers  24
Malta War Memorial  25
Mercantile Marine First World War  26
Merchant Seamens Second World War  28
St Michael Cornhill War Memorial  29
Victims of Oppression  30
**London EC4**
National Firefighters Memorial  31
National Submariners' War Memorial  32
**London N1**
Islington Green War Memorial  33
**London N3**
La Delivrance  34
**London N5**
Boer War Memorial  35
**London N8**
Hornsey War Memorial  36

**London N12**
Men Of Finchley  37
**London N22**
Wood Green War Memorial  38
**London NW1**
London and North Western Railway War Memorial  39
**London NW2**
Prisoners of War & Concentration Camps  40
**London SE1**
International Brigade Spanish Civil War  41
St Saviours Southwark War Memorial  42
Soviet War Memorial  43
Victory Arch Waterloo Railway Station  44
Violet Szabo and SOE Agents  45
**London SE11**
Following the Leader  46
**London SE16**
22nd Battalion, The London Regiment  47
**London SW1**
Australian War Memorial  48
Bali Bombings Memorial  49
Battle of Britain Monument  50
Boadicea/ Boudica  52
Cadiz Memorial  53
Canadian Memorial  54
Cenotaph  55
Chindit Memorial  56
Combined Forces Memorial  57
Commonwealth Memorial Gates  58
Crimea and Indian Mutiny  59
Fleet Air Arm Memorial  60
The Guards memorial  61
The Guards Crimean War Memorial  62
Gurkha Memorial  63
Iraq and Afghanistan Memorial  64
Korean War Memorial  65
Rifle Brigade War Memorial  66
Royal Air Force Memorial  67
Royal Artillery Memorial  68
Royal Artillery Memorial - Boer War  70
Royal Marines National Memorial  71
Royal Naval Division Memorial  72
Royal Tank Regiment Memorial  73
Unknown Warrior  74
Women of World War II  75

**London SW2**
African and Caribbean War Memorial  76
**London SW3**
6th Dragoon Guards (The Carabiniers)  77
**London SW6**
Fulham War Memorial  78
Fulham (All Saints) War Memorial  78
**London SW7**
Communist Victims/Twelve Responses to Tragedy  79
**London SW11**
24th East Surrey Division  80
**London W1**
7th July Memorial  81
Animals in War Memorial  82
Cavalry of the Empire Memorial  84
Eagle Squadrons Memorial  85
Machine Gun Corps Memorial  86
Marylebone War Memorial  87
New Zealand War Memorial  88
RAF Bomber Command  90
**London W2**
Great Western Railway War Memorial  92
Lancaster Gate Memorial Cross  93
**London W3**
Katyn Massacre Memorial  94
**London W4**
Bedford Park War Memorial  95
**London W8**
Kensington War Memorial  96
**London W12**
War Memorial Shepherds Bush  97
**London WC1**
Medical Men & Women  98
Rangers 12th County of London Regiment  99
**London WC2**
Belgian Monument to the British Nation  100
Civil Service Rifles War Memorial  101
Edith Cavell Memorial 102
Imperial Camel Corps 103
Lincolns Inn (Inns of Court Regiment) Memorial  104

**Barking & Dagenham**
Barking Park War Memorial  105
**Barnet**
New Barnet (East Barnet Valley)War Memorial  106
**Bexley**
Bexley War Memorial  107
**Bromley**
Bromley War Memorial  108
**Croydon**
Croydon Aerodrome Battle of Britain Memorial  109
Croydon Cenotaph  110
**Enfield**
Enfield War Memorial  111
**Harrow**
Harrow on the Hill War Memorial  112
Harrow School War Memorial Building & Shrine  113
**Havering**
Rainham War Memorial  114
**Hillingdon**
Harefield War Memorial  115
Polish War Memorial  116
**Hounslow**
Heston War Memorial  118
**Kingston upon Thames**
Kingston upon Thames WW1 & WW2 Memorial 119
**Richmond upon Thames**
Bromhead Memorial  120
South African War Memorial  121
The Cross of Sacrifice  122
**Sutton**
Sutton War Memorial  123

ALPHABETICAL INDEX  124

# INTRODUCTION

There are an estimated 100,000 war memorials in the UK. Every city, town and village has some form of memorial to commemorate the dead. For centuries, people have mourned and memorialised in many different ways.

This book takes a close visual look at the huge variety of memorials that exist in London. They take many forms, including cenotaphs, monuments, plaques, gardens, crosses, buildings and rolls of honour. They range from the traditional to the modern, some are big imposing monuments, whilst others are small and modest rolls of honour.

As a photographer it was my aim to produce a book of contemporary photographs which emphasise the details and aesthetic value of each monument. Most of the monuments in this book are located in central London but also included are several in the Greater London area.

Central London differs from the rest of the country in that there are a large number of memorials dating back through the centuries which are situated within a small area. These are dedicated to Regiments, individuals, wars and specific groups of individuals as well as memorials to those who lost their lives during terrorist attacks.

After the end of the First World War, memorials began to appear in different locations of London, not just in the capital's most important churches or prestigious sites. During the war Londoners from all walks of life volunteered, and conscription took people from all parts of society, from the poorest neighborhoods, to the richest sons of the aristocracy. Battalions were formed from friends or workmates from particular areas. People joined in groups from the same factory and the same close-knit communities. This book includes memorials erected to commemorate all these groups of people.

Many of the memorials have listed status by English Heritage (an explanation of grading criteria is on the following page) which gives them legal protection against demolition or modification and requires permission from the local planning authority. Those that have listing status in this book are shown with the Grade mentioned first in the text.

*Barbara Glebska*

# The following is an explanation of the grading and criteria for listing a building or structure. Taken from the website www.historicengland.org.uk

Buildings and structures are assessed to define their significance with the greatest care. Many old buildings and recent buildings are interesting, but listing identifies only those which are of national 'special interest'. The main criteria used are:
- **Age and rarity:** most buildings built before 1700 which survive in anything like their original condition are listed, as are most of those built between 1700 and 1840
- **Architectural interest:** buildings which are nationally important for the interest of their architectural design, decoration and craftsmanship; also important examples of particular building types and techniques
- **Historic interest:** this includes buildings which illustrate important aspects of the nation's social, economic, cultural or military history
- **Close historical association** with nationally important people or events
- **Group value,** especially where buildings are part of an important architectural or historic group or are a fine example of planning (such as squares, terraces and model villages)

The criteria become tighter with time, so that buildings built within the last 30 years have to be exceptionally important to be listed, and under threat too. Particularly careful selection is required for buildings from the period after 1945. A building has normally to be over 30 years old to be eligible for listing.

## Categories of listed buildings

- **Grade I** buildings are of exceptional interest, only 2.5% of listed buildings are Grade I
- **Grade II\*** buildings are particularly important buildings of more than special interest; 5.5% of listed buildings are Grade II\*
- **Grade II** buildings are of special interest; 92% of all listed buildings are in this class and it is the most likely grade of listing for a home owner.

In England there are approximately 376,099 listed building entries (as of March 2015).
The total number of listed buildings is not known, as one single entry can sometimes cover a number of individual units, such as a listed terrace of houses. The total is thought to be around 500,000.

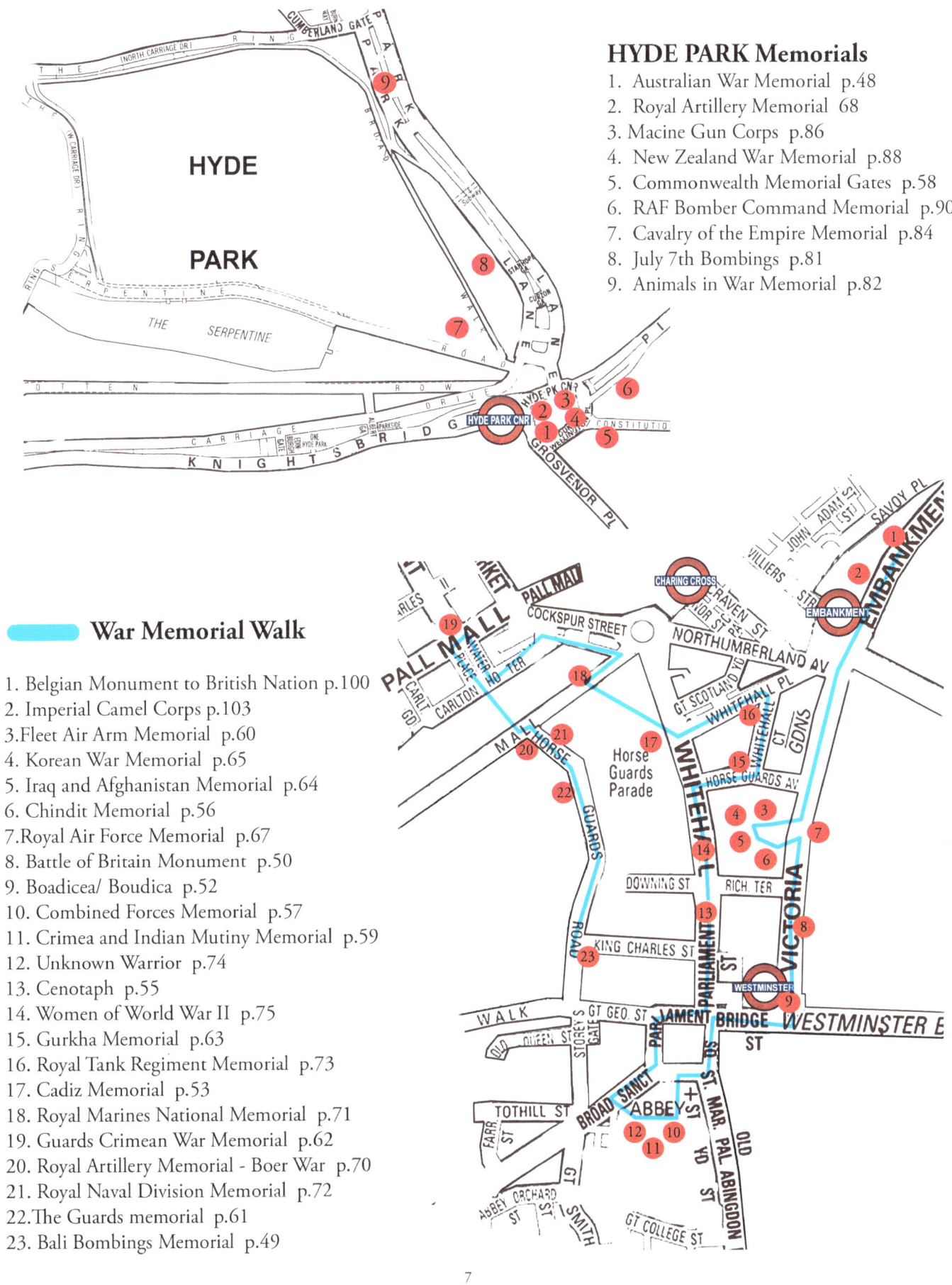

## HYDE PARK Memorials

1. Australian War Memorial p.48
2. Royal Artillery Memorial 68
3. Macine Gun Corps p.86
4. New Zealand War Memorial p.88
5. Commonwealth Memorial Gates p.58
6. RAF Bomber Command Memorial p.90
7. Cavalry of the Empire Memorial p.84
8. July 7th Bombings p.81
9. Animals in War Memorial p.82

## War Memorial Walk

1. Belgian Monument to British Nation p.100
2. Imperial Camel Corps p.103
3. Fleet Air Arm Memorial p.60
4. Korean War Memorial p.65
5. Iraq and Afghanistan Memorial p.64
6. Chindit Memorial p.56
7. Royal Air Force Memorial p.67
8. Battle of Britain Monument p.50
9. Boadicea/ Boudica p.52
10. Combined Forces Memorial p.57
11. Crimea and Indian Mutiny Memorial p.59
12. Unknown Warrior p.74
13. Cenotaph p.55
14. Women of World War II p.75
15. Gurkha Memorial p.63
16. Royal Tank Regiment Memorial p.73
17. Cadiz Memorial p.53
18. Royal Marines National Memorial p.71
19. Guards Crimean War Memorial p.62
20. Royal Artillery Memorial - Boer War p.70
21. Royal Naval Division Memorial p.72
22. The Guards memorial p.61
23. Bali Bombings Memorial p.49

# LONDON E1

## Memorial to the Civilians of East London

HERMITAGE RIVERSIDE MEMORIAL GARDEN E1

On the low, large square plinth there are two texts repeated on opposite sides, inscribed with golden lettering:
2nd WORLD WAR 1939 - 45
MEMORIAL TO THE CIVILIANS OF EAST LONDON
On a nearby information panel:
The Hermitage Memorial Riverside Garden
'The garden and memorial sculpture are in memory of the East London civilians who were killed and injured in the Second World War, 1939 - 1945, and of the suffering of those who lost relatives, friends and homes.
Tens of thousands of men, women and children lost life and limb in the wartime bombing of London and other major cities. More than a million homes were destroyed.
The most intense bombing occurred between September 1940 and May 1941 and became known as the Blitz (from the German "Blitzkrieg" meaning "lightning war").
In the first three months of the Blitz bombs rained on London almost every night.
The Port of London, with its docks, warehouses and industry, was an important strategic target for the German bombers and an easy one to locate along the Thames. Countless bombs also fell on the surrounding densely packed streets of East and South East London, which were home to many of London's poorest families. The consequences were devastating. On this site stood the Hermitage Wharf, which was hit during a massive firebomb raid on the City of London on 29 December 1940.
The memorial sculpture was designed by Wendy Taylor CBE. The symbol of the dove is intended to suggest hope, rather than dwell intrusively on the dead. Its representation as an absence signifies the loved ones who were lost.
Unveiled by the then Communities Secretary MP Hazel Blears and Alf Roffey who had been a fire-watcher in Wapping during the Blitz.'

# LONDON E2

## Stairway to Heaven, Bethnal Green Memorial
UNNAMED ROAD E2

Inscription on plaque: The Bethnal Green Tube Shelter Disaster.
On 3 March 1943 the air raid warning sounded at 8.17pm. People made their way in the pitch dark of the blackout to file in an orderly manner down the steps of the single entrance to the unfinished Bethnal Green underground station next to this memorial. It had been in regular use since 1940 as a deep air raid shelter.

Over the next 10 minutes local pubs and cinemas emptied so that some 2000 people were already in the shelter by 8.27pm when the searchlight went on. Those still waiting to enter were alarmed by the deafening sound of a new anti-aircraft rocket battery opening fire for the first time nearby. They assumed it to be enemy bombs falling. At that time three buses set down their passengers at the unsupervised shelter entrance. The crowd hurried down the poorly-lit 10 foot wide first flight of 19 concrete steps which had no central handrail. On this wet, slippery stairway a woman with a child fell on the 3rd step from the bottom and others tumbled over her. The crowd above continued pressing forward unable to see the horror of what was happening below. Within seconds the whole staircase was a solid, tangled mass of 300 people trapped five or six deep.

Despite heroic efforts, rescuers working above and below found it difficult to release them before they suffocated in the crush. It was 11.40pm before the last of the total 173 dead was pulled out – 84 women, 62 children and 27 men. Sixty-two people were hospitalised and at least 30 more walked away wounded. Many more suffered life-long trauma. This was the worst civilian disaster of the Second World War.

Titled the "Stairway to Heaven". Unveiled in 2017 designed by Harry Paticas. Large abstract sculptural structure of mixed materials including stone, metal and teak. Three plaques list 173 names of all those who died in the civilian disaster. The design incorporates a teak staircase with 173 conicals, each to represent a victim. Scattered across the top surface of the monument are 15 other plaques, each giving some details about an individual victim or the remembrances of a survivor.

## Gas workers war memorial
IMPERIAL GAS LIGHT AND COKE COMPANY MEMORIAL GARDENS, TWELVETREES CRESCENT, BROMLEY-BY-BOW E3 3TE

GRADE: II Three war memorials in a small park adjacent to the former London Gas Museum, and the Bromley-by-Bow gas works. The memorials commemorate the employees of Gas Light & Coke Company, who perished in the two World Wars.

Memorial comprises a stone column surmounted with flat capital on which sits a tall iron-framed and glass octagonal gas lamp which evokes the 'eternal flame' and links it closely to the history of this important company. This is set on a stone base, rectangular in plan, which formerly held two bronze plaques commemorating the many employees killed in World Wars I and II. These included ceramic tiles with the arms of the company, featuring a pair of salamanders breathing fire.

Adjacent to this are two structures, that carry duplicate plaques. One is in the form of a rotunda. A circle of columns with seating in between and an ornate wrought iron dome above. At centre of structure is a stone block bearing two plaques, one for each of the world wars. WW1 plaque has an angel relief dressed in armour with sword. WW2 plaque has coat of arms in top left corner.
Inscription Upper plaque: THESE MEN DIED FOR THEIR COUNTRY/ (Names)
1914-1919 THE GAS LIGHT AND COKE COMPANY.
Lower plaque: TO THE MEMORY OF THOSE MEMBERS OF THE COMPANY WHO GAVE THEIR LIVES IN THE WAR OF 1939-1945 REQUIESCANT IN PACE./ (Names)

# LONDON E4

## Chingford War Memorial

THE RIDGEWAY E4

GRADE: II The Chingford War Memorial was commissioned by public subscription to commemorate the 242 local men who fell in the First World War. It was designed by WA Lewis and unveiled in 1921.
Following the Second World War a further inscription was added devoted to the casualties of World War II, and a modern plaque has been added commemorating those victims of conflict up to the present day.
Constructed from granite, with an octagonal stepped paved base, the memorial stands in a paved area within a small garden at an intersection on the edge of the former village.

Inscription: 'IN GRATEFUL REMEMBRANCE OF THE MEN OF CHINGFORD WHO DIED IN THE SERVICE OF THEIR COUNTRY IN THE GREAT WAR 1914-1918 "WE ARE THE DEAD..... TO YOU FROM FAILING HANDS WE THROW THE TORCH BE YOURS TO HOLD IT HIGH",   'AND OF THOSE WHO LOST THEIR LIVES 1939 – 1945'.
'IN MEMORY OF THE FALLEN OF CHINGFORD 1945 TO PRESENT DAY, LEST WE FORGET".
The other sides of the plinth are inscribed with the names of the 242 fallen soldiers from WWI.

# LONDON E6

## East Ham War Memorial,
CENTRAL PARK
HIGH STREET SOUTH E6

GRADE: II Erected in 1921 to commemorate the many men of East Ham who fell during the First World War. The memorial was designed by the architect Robert Banks-Martin, who was the mayor of East Ham during the war. The Roll of Honour is spread between the four sides of the memorial and contains a total of 1824 names.

Cenotaph with domed pediment supported by four pillars and enclosing a decorative pinnacle. Panels on all four sides. Whole is mounted on a three stepped base. A bronze wreath is mounted between the two pillars at the front and rear faces.

Inscription: THIS MONUMENT IS ERECTED TO THE GLORY OF GOD AND IN MEMORY OF EAST HAM'S BRAVEST SONS WHO FELL IN THE GREAT WAR 1914 - 1918 32ND (S) EAST HAM BATTALION THE ROYAL FUSILIERS NOVEMBER 1915 MARCH 1918 PLOEGSTRAETE PASSCHAENDALE SOMME VIERSTRAAT ITALY NIEUPORT MESSINES

IN MEMORY OF THE OFFICERS NON COMMISSIONED OFFICERS AND MEN OF THE 32ND (S) EAST HAM BATTALION THE ROYAL FUSILIERS WHO GAVE THEIR LIVES IN THE GREAT WAR 1914 - 1918 THIS TABLET IS DEDICATED BY THE OFFICERS NON-COMMISSIONED OFFICERS AND MEN OF THE 141ST (EAST HAM) HEAVY BATTERY ROYAL GARRISON ARTILLERY TO THE MEMORY OF THEIR COMRADES WHO MADE THE SUPREME SACRIFICE DURING THE GREAT WAR

# LONDON E8

## St John at Hackney War Memorial
ST JOHN AT HACKNEY CHURCHYARD GARDENS, LOWER CLAPTON ROAD E8

GRADE: II War memorial 1921 by Hermon Cawthra commemorates the men of Hackney who served and died in WWI and WWII. Portland stone obelisk with bronze robed figure of a knight, holding sword and wreath.
The upper level bears the inscription: COURAGE SACRIFICE
A stone plaque at the base of the pillar is inscribed: TO THE GLORY OF GOD AND TO THE HONOURED MEMORY OF THE MEN OF THIS BOROUGH WHO MADE THE SUPREME SACRIFICE DURING THE GREAT WAR OF 1914 - 1918
The south side has a wreath surrounding a burning torch carved in the stone work.
A stone plaque at the base of the pillar is inscribed: THE HOUSES IN WATTISFORD ROAD MILLFIELDS ERECTED FOR THE USE OF DISABLED SAILORS AND SOLDIERS ARE A FURTHER TRIBUTE OF THE BOROUGH TO THE MEMORY OF THE FALLEN
A stone plaque at the base of the west side of the pillar is inscribed: TO THE GLORY OF GOD AND TO THE HONOURED MEMORY OF THE MEN OF THIS BOROUGH WHO MADE THE SUPREME SACRIFICE DURING THE GREAT WAR OF 1939 - 1945
The almshouses in Wattisford Road for Disabled Soldiers and Sailors, referred to in the inscription, were opened in 1923. They consist of a row of six cottages with a semi-detached house at each end.

# LONDON E14

## War memorial to the Children of Upper North Street School
POPLAR RECREATION GROUND
EAST INDIA DOCK ROAD E14

GRADE II* The memorial marks the deaths of 18 children in the German air-raid over London by Gotha aircraft, a raid which caused the single highest number of casualties of all the air-raids on the city.

German air-raids on Britain during the First World War began in early 1915, when Zeppelins were used. In May 1917 the first raids using Gotha bombers began. These bombers were aircraft capable of long-distance flights, and were used to make day-light raids.

On 13 June 1917, a squadron of the German Army High Command created specifically for bombing England, flew from Belgium to attack the City of London. The attack resulted in 162 civilian deaths and injury to a further 432 people.

Amongst the dead were 18 children from Upper North Street School, Poplar. A bomb dropped by a Gotha on its return from the City raid passed through the school roof and the upper stories, exploding in the classroom below where more than 60 Infants were being taught. Of the 18 children who died, 16 were aged five or six years. At least 37 other children were injured, some very seriously.

The children were buried at a funeral on 20 June, three in private interments and the rest in a mass grave in East London Cemetery.

The tall stone memorial comprises an angel in mourning, wings outstretched with clasped hands, standing on a three-staged Gothic structure. The upper stage takes the form of a hooded shrine. The arch of the front face is decorated with floral carvings in low relief, whilst the panel below has a roundel enclosing the seal of Poplar Borough Council.

The inscription reads IN MEMORY OF 18 CHILDREN WHO WERE KILLED BY A BOMB DROPPED FROM A GERMAN AEROPLANE UPON THE L.C.C. SCHOOL UPPER NORTH STREET POPLAR ON THE 13TH OF JUNE 1917. ALFRED H. WARREN O.B.E. MAYOR J. BUTEUX SKEGGS, TOWN CLERK.

The commemorated names are listed on the side faces, recording the name and age of each child.

The middle stage in a white stone comprises three steps supporting the shrine. An inscription on the middle step reads ERECTED BY PUBLIC SUBSCRIPTION with below A.R. ADAMS/ POPLAR.

# LONDON E17

**Walthamstow War Memorial**  WALTHAM FOREST TOWN HALL, FOREST ROAD E17

GRADE: II 1922, free-standing stone memorial to the fallen of the First World War with later inscriptions commemorating the Second World War and subsequent conflicts. A stepped plinth surmounted by a neo-classical canopy of four Ionic columns supporting an entablature.
Inscription 'OUR GLORIOUS DEAD "LEST WE FORGET" 1914-1918 1939-1945', with a low relief moulded heraldic shield. Plaque inscribed ' IN MEMORY OF THE FALLEN OF WALTHAMSTOW 1945 TO THE PRESENT DAY'. A sculpture of a mourning woman in classical robes stands on the stepped base, leaning on the plinth with her head bowed.

# LONDON EC1

## Postal Workers' War Memorial
MOUNT PLEASANT MAIL CENTRE, FARRINGDON ROAD EC1

GRADE: II  War memorial erected 1920 and moved to its present site in 2013.

The First and Second World Wars often had an extreme impact on particular communities; this memorial illustrates that impact on the Western Postal District.

The memorial, commemorating London's Western District postal workers who fell in the First World War, was erected in 1920 at the Wimpole Street Post Office. Funds were raised from the staff of the district.

When the post office closed in 1981 the memorial was moved to the delivery offices at Rathbone Place, and then, on its closure in 2013 to the sorting offices and postal museum at Mount Pleasant.

The memorial is in the form of an aedicule with Ionic columns and a broken semi-circular pediment. It frames a stone tablet inscribed with the names of 130 men. Within the tympanum is a gilt wreath and sword, inscribed within: 'PRO PATRIA  ET LIBERTATE; a plaque beneath is inscribed: TO THE HONOURED MEMORY OF OUR HEROIC COMRADES WHO FELL IN THE GREAT WAR 1914-1919.

The base is inscribed: 'SUBSCRIBED FOR AND ERECTED BY THEIR COLLEAGUES OF THE WESTERN POSTAL DISTRICT AS A LASTING TRIBUTE TO THEIR SELF-SACRIFICE'. The plinth has a metal plaque commemorating those lost in the Second World War, inscribed '1939-1945' with the names of 56 men.

# LONDON EC1

## Prudential War Memorial
WATERHOUSE SQUARE
HOLBORN EC1

Memorial to the 786 Prudential employees who fell in the Great War. Sculptor F.V. Blundstone RBS Unveiled in1922.

Two life sized winged female figures cradling a dying soldier, representing a clerk of the establishment. Four half draped figures of women representing the three services and national service stand at the corners of a square pedestal. Two small bas reliefs under the top of the pedestal depict ships of war and dying soldiers. Plaques inscribed with the names of the fallen are mounted on the pedestal.

Inscription IN MEMORY OF THE GLORIOUS SACRIFICE OFFERED BY PRUDENTIAL MEN WHO FELL IN THE GREAT WAR 1914 - 1919 WE ARE BOUND TO GIVE THANKS ALWAY TO GOD FOR YOU BRETHEREN BELOVED OF THE LORD FOR YE ARE OUR GLORY AND JOY

Prudential Second World War Panels, 1950 Sculptor F.V. Blundstone RBS Blundstone's second memorial for the central office is in two parts. One panel lists names A-K, the second K-Z. Each is topped with a figure of St George on top.

# LONDON EC1

## Royal Fusiliers War Memorial
HIGH HOLBORN EC1

GRADE: II*  Erected 1922, after the First World War, to the design of architects Cheadle and Harding and sculptor Albert Toft. Portland stone pedestal, bronze plaques and a bronze figure. Further inscriptions added after the Second World War.

The Royal Fusiliers War Memorial was erected in 1922 in memory of the 21,941 Royal Fusiliers who died during the First World War. This included those men of the 45th and 46th Battalions who lost their lives in 1919 during the North Russia Intervention. It also stands as a memorial to fusiliers that fell during the Second World War and subsequent conflicts.

The regiment served in numerous conflicts, including: the Napoleonic Wars, the Crimean War, Second Boer War, the First World War and the Second World War.

The memorial comprises a 2.6m high bronze statue surmounting a 5m high tapered Portland Stone pedestal and chamfered base. The statue is a private infantry soldier of the Royal Fusiliers in full service dress; boots, puttee, uniform, knapsack, ammunition pouches, backpack and helmet, carrying a rifle with a fixed bayonet behind him in his right hand. He stands with his head turned and his right leg raised on a rock, as having climbed to a vantage point to scan the horizon. His left hand is clenched in a fist in front of him and he faces directly along the road to the west to guard the entrance to the City of London. On the front side of the pedestal is the regimental badge: a Tudor rose enclosed by the Garter bearing the motto: HONI SOIT QUI MAL Y PENSE ('shame on him with evil thoughts'), surmounted by a King's crown.

Beneath the badge is the inscription: THE ROYAL FUSILIERS (CITY OF LONDON REGIMENT) TO THE GLORIOUS MEMORY OF THE 22,000 ROYAL FUSILIERS WHO FELL IN THE GREAT WAR 1914-1919 AND TO THE ROYAL FUSILIERS WHO FELL IN THE WORLD WAR 1939-1945.

On the chamfered top of the base is a stone block, inserted at a later date, inscribed in small lettering: AND THOSE FUSILIERS KILLED IN SUBSEQUENT CAMPAIGNS. The rear side of the pedestal has a bronze plaque bearing a list of the 53 regular, service, and territorial battalions of the regiment that served in the First World War.

# LONDON EC2

### Great Eastern Railway War Memorial — LIVERPOOL STREET STATION EC2

The Great Eastern Railway War Memorial unveiled in 1922. Large ornate marble wall plaque. Roll of honour 1108 names on 11 panels surmounted by segmental pediment with relief of laurel and the Great Eastern Railway coat of arms. On the wall below the large war memorial are smaller memorials to Wilson, and to Captain Charles Fryatt, an officer of the Great Eastern Railway's marine service who was executed by the Germans in 1916 after being convicted at a court martial as a franc-tireur.

Inscription: TO THE GLORY OF GOD AND IN GRATEFUL MEMORY OF THE GREAT EASTERN RAILWAY STAFF WHO IN RESPONSE TO THE CALL OF THEIR KING AND COUNTRY, SACRIFICED THEIR LIVES DURING THE GREAT WAR 1914-1919

# LONDON EC2

## Kindertransport - the arrival
HOPE SQUARE, LIVERPOOL STREET STATION EC2

'Kindertransport - the arrival' unveiled in 2006 is one of three memorials at Liverpool Street Station in London, where trains of children fleeing from Nazi tyranny arrived in England. From here, the children were sent to foster homes and hostels.

Around the base of the memorial are bronze blocks listing the cities from which children fled: Cologne, Hanover, Nuremberg, Stuttgart, Dusseldorf, Frankfurt, Bremen, Munich, Danzig, Breslau, Prague, Hamburg, Mannheim, Leipzig, Berlin, Vienna.

Kindertranpsort– the arrival is part of a series of four sculptures which have been erected along the children's route to safety. The others by the same sculptor being 'Kindertransport – the departure' in Danzig, Poland, 'Trains to life – trains to death' at Friedrichstraße railway station, Berlin and 'Channel of life' at the hook of Holland, Rotterdam. Frank Meisler the scultor was himself a passenger on a Kindertransport train and was awarded the "Freedom of the City of London" for his work on these memorials.

The plaque reads:
CHILDREN OF THE KINDERTRANSPORT
IN GRATITUDE TO THE PEOPLE OF BRITAIN FOR SAVING THE LIVES OF 10,000 UNACCOMPANIED MAINLY JEWISH CHILDREN WHO FLED FROM NAZI PERSECUTION IN 1938 AND 1939
"WHOSOEVER RESCUES A SINGLE SOUL IS CREDITED AS THOUGH THEY HAD SAVED THE WHOLE WORLD" Talmud.

# City and County of London Troops War Memorial
CORNHILL EC3

GRADE: II*  A First World War regimental memorial, 1920, with added post-Second World War inscription. Sculptor Alfred Drury, architect Sir Aston Webb.

The City and County of London Troops memorial stands at the heart of the City of London and reflects the London units as they were constituted at the end of the First World War. A number of the battalions were originally raised by specific localities or communities and though many of the units represented also instituted their own war memorials for fallen comrades, this memorial commemorates all those men and women who served in the City and County of London Troops.

Portland stone pier and plinths, granite base, bronze statuary. Approximately 7.5m high, it comprises a finely detailed Portland stone pier with two rounded buttress plinths to the base, each of which supports the life-sized bronze statue of a soldier.

The front face of the central pier bears a carving in relief of the coat of arms of the City of London, above three dedicatory inscriptions reading:
TO THE IMMORTAL HONOUR OF THE OFFICERS NON-COMMISSIONED OFFICERS AND MEN OF LONDON WHO SERVED THEIR KING AND EMPIRE IN THE GREAT WAR 1914 - 1919 THIS MEMORIAL IS DEDICATED IN PROUD & GRATEFUL RECOGNITION BY THE CITY AND COUNTY OF LONDON THEIR NAME LIVETH FOR EVERMORE
UNVEILED ON NOV 12TH 1920 BY HRH THE DUKE OF YORK

ON BEHALF OF FIELD-MARSHAL HRH THE DUKE OF CONNAUGHT K.G., K.T., K.P. AND ALBEIT MANY UNITS NAMED HEREON HAVE CHANGED IN DESIGNATION AND ROLE WE HONOUR AND REMEMBER THE MEN AND WOMEN WHO SERVED IN ALL THE UNITS OF THE CITY AND COUNTY OF LONDON IN THE WAR OF 1939-1945.

Below this an inscription on a small bronze plaque, added after 1945 when the Second World War dedication above replaced the original record, reads RAISED BY PUBLIC SUBSCRIPTION AT THE MANSION HOUSE IN THE PEACE YEAR 1919 DURING THE MAYORALTY OF COL THE RT. HON SIR HORACE BROOKS MARSHALL K.C.V.O. LL.D.

Around the base two rows of bronze pegs ornamented with crossed rifles carry chains for the suspension of wreaths. On the rear of the central pier is displayed the heavily mantled coat of arms of the County of London, below which is the list of the commemorated units.

Each side of the pier bears carvings in low relief of three standards, each surmounted by a wreathed crown and topped with a lion statant guardant. On the left buttress stands the bronze statue of a Royal Artilleryman, standing at ease with his rifle in his right hand.

On the right buttress stands the corresponding bronze statue of a Royal Fusilier, standing easy with both hands resting on the muzzle of his rifle.

The corniced top of the pier is surmounted by a moulded stone pedestal on which stands a bronze of a lion holding a shield. The shield is ornamented with a relief of St George, mounted, killing a dragon with the legend
ST GEORGE FOR ENGLAND.

*Above:* Statue of Royal Artilleryman

*Below:* Statue of Royal Fusilier

*Right:* The rear of the central pier

# LONDON EC3

## Falklands Merchant Seafarers
TRINITY GARDENS, TOWER HILL EC3

Memorial dedicated to members of the Royal Fleet Auxiliary and Merchant Seamen who lost their lives in the Falklands Campaign. Designed by Gordon Newton. The theme of the memorial was chosen to be "Time and Distance" which is represented by a sundial whose base is a compass rose with a bronze anchor and chain forming the gnomon. The compass points were manufactured from polished black granite and the base is made of Portland stone with bronze panels containing the names of the Merchant Navy and RFA casualties and their ships. The memorial was dedicated on Merchant Navy Day 4 September 2005.

Inscription large plaque: IN MEMORY OF THOSE MERCHANT SEAFARERS WHO GAVE THEIR LIVES TO SECURE THE FREEDOM OF THE FALKLAND ISLANDS 1982

The other two plaques carry the names of the 17 Merchant Navy and RFA casualties and their ships - SS ATLANTIC CONVEYOR LIVERPOOL: RFA SIR GALAHAD LONDON: RFA FORT GRANGE LONDON: RFA SIR TRISTRAM LONDON

# LONDON EC3

## Malta War Memorial
ALL HALLOWS BY THE TOWER CHURCH
BYWARD STREET EC3

A memorial to the brave people of Malta and the island that was awarded a George Cross. During World War II, Malta was under the protection of England. Malta was surrounded by the Axis Forces, and it became the most bombed place in the history of the war.

Inscription: Malta G.C. The Siege of 1940-43  In 1940 the sinister shadow of Fascism spilled across Europe and into North Africa.  Malta, under the protection of Great Britain, found herself alone in a hostile Mediterranean 800 miles from her nearest allies in Gibraltar and Alexandria.  Besieged by enemies Malta became a fulcrum on which the fate of the war balanced for the next three years.  If Malta fell the rest of North Africa would follow, opening the door to the oil fields of the Middle East and for the Axis Powers to join in Asia and threaten India.  The allies knew this.  So did the Axis Powers.  Malta, besieged, became and remains the most bombed place in the history of War.

Supplied only by Sea, at great cost, Malta was defended not only by her own people but by forces drawn from the whole free world.  Fighter aircraft delivered by the American and Royal Navies were piloted by Britons, Canadians, Australians, and New Zealanders.  Convoys crewed by British, American and Commonwealth seamen were supported by the free forces of Greece, the Netherlands, and Poland.  Free Norwegians added their merchant fleet to the Allied cause. In April 1942 King George VI awarded to the People of Malta the George Cross, the highest decoration for civilian courage and heroism.

By summer 1942 only weeks of food remained and the Allies mounted operation Pedestal as a last attempt to save Malta. After a five-day running battle the Convoy's four remaining merchant vessels and the immortal Tanker Ohio, all that was left of the fourteen that set out, entered Grand Harbour. The date was 15th August, 1942, the feast of Santa Maria. The siege was broken; within months North Africa was retaken and the first steps of European liberation begun.

This stone taken from Malta, was presented by the Maltese Government on the 60th Anniversary of the end of Second World War to commemorate all who participated in the siege and defence of Malta, 1940-43. Placed by the George Cross Island Association, 15th August 2005.

The west face of the monument carries a map showing the "Theatre of operations of the Mediterranean Fleet".
On the east face: The Governor, Malta. To honour her brave people I award the George Cross to the island fortress of

Malta to bear witness to a heroism and devotion that will long be famous in history. George RI April 15th 1942
The citation from King George VI to the Governor of Malta. Below an icon showing a shield with the Stars and Stripes and the Union Jack: "In the name of people of the United States of America I salute the island of Malta, its people and defenders, who, in the cause of freedom and justice and decency throughout the world, have rendered valourous service far and above the call of duty.  Under repeated fire from the skies, Malta stood alone but unafraid in the center of the sea, one tiny, bright flame in the darkness - - a beacon of hope for the clearer days which have come.  Malta's bright story of human fortitude and courage will be read by posterity with wonder and gratitude through all the ages. What was done in this island maintains the highest traditions of gallant men and women who from the beginning of time have lived and died to preserve civilization for all mankind." Franklin D. Roosevelt  7th December 1943  The tribute read by President Roosevelt when he visited Malta.
The north face carries a detailed time-line of the siege.

# LONDON EC3

## The Mercantile Marine First World War Memorial  TRINITY SQUARE GARDENS, TOWER HILL EC3

GRADE: I  First World War memorial by Sir Edwin Landseer Lutyens to the missing of the Merchant Navy and Fishing Fleet, 1928. Sculpture by Sir William Reid-Dick. Portland stone with bronze plaques, wrought iron gates. The memorial, raised on a platform above street level, is in the form of a temple of three bays. Each bay is formed of piers and columns in the long side walls, flanking the central open space. The piers forming the bays have external round arch curved niches in Portland stone, and are clad in rectangular bronze panels laid in a stretcher bond pattern and giving the appearance of rusticated walling. These panels bear the names of the missing, arranged by vessel. Bronze security spikes are fixed in the wall openings to the southern elevation. To the centre is a square, stepped, attic.

The principal dedicatory inscription, in bronze reads 1914-1918 TO THE GLORY OF GOD AND TO THE HONOUR OF TWELVE THOUSAND OF THE MERCHANT NAVY AND FISHING FLEETS WHO HAVE NO GRAVE BUT THE SEA.

The temple is floored with black and white chequerboard stone paving. A flight of five stone steps, with iron gates, leads up from the street at either end of the temple and from the platform further steps lead down into the garden and Second World War memorial.

During the First World War, a duty of the Merchant Navy was to be a supply service of the Royal Navy. This role included troop transportation, delivering supplies to the armed forces, shipping raw materials to overseas factories and bringing back the completed products, including munitions, and supplying personnel and ships for military service. It was also vital that the Merchant Navy continued its peacetime role, supplying food and goods to the home nation, import and export shipping, and that the fishing fleet continued to bring catches into British ports.

Losses to civilian shipping were high from the outset of the First World War, but peaked in 1917 following the German government's announcement of unrestricted submarine warfare. The Ministry of Shipping was responsible for establishing preventative measures to deal with the underwater threat. These included the convoy system, in which warships were employed as escorts to merchant fleets.

Nevertheless, 3,305 merchant ships were lost during the First World War, at the loss of some 17,000 lives. These included individuals from around the Empire, manning the diverse vessels of the merchant fleet.

The memorial commemorates some 12,000 named casualties. It was unveiled on 12 December 1928 by Queen Mary.

# LONDON EC3

## Merchant Seamens Second World War Memorial — TRINITY SQUARE GARDENS, TOWER HILL, EC3

GRADE: II* Second World War memorial unveiled in 1955 designed by Edward Maufe as a complement to the adjoining First World War memorial. The sculptor was Charles Wheeler. Portland stone walls set with bronze panels recalling the names of those who have no known grave. The 8ft walls set in a sunken garden are lined with bronze panels and spaced at set intervals with seven stone sculptured allegorical figures representing the seven seas. At the centre of this garden is a 'pool' of bronze engraved as a Mariners' compass and set to magnetic north. Steps ascend to the earlier war memorial, between pylons carved with above life-size figures of an officer and seaman of the merchant service. Inscription reads 1939 - 1945 THE TWENTY-FOUR THOUSAND OF THE MERCHANT NAVY AND FISHING FLEETS WHOSE NAMES ARE HONOURED ON THE WALLS OF THIS GARDEN, GAVE THEIR LIVES FOR THEIR COUNTRY AND HAVE NO GRAVE BUT THE SEA. The Tower Hill Memorial commemorates all merchant seamen who served in ships registered in ports of the British commonwealth or in ships on charter to these governments, who lost their lives as a result of enemy action. 23,765 men are commemorated, including 80 pilots and lighthousemen and 832 fishermen.

# London EC3

## St Michael Cornhill War Memorial
ST MICHAEL'S ALLEY
CORNHILL EC3

GRADE: II* First World War memorial. 1920. Sculptor Richard Goulden. The memorial commemorates the City employees who worked within the parish of St Michael Cornhill. The names of the fallen are recorded separately on a framed Roll of Honour inside the church. More than 2,000 men had volunteered for military service during the First World War, of whom c170 died.

The war memorial abuts the western pier of the porch of the Church. The pier dates from Sir George Gilbert Scott's 1857-60 remodelling of the Wren church and forms the lowest stage of the tall Gothic tower of 1715-22. The memorial consists of a narrow, tapering Portland stone pedestal on a deep plinth.

Above is a bronze sculptural group surmounted by the youthful figure of St Michael the Archangel, the parish church's patron saint and symbol of the triumph of good over evil. The Archangel, wings upstretched, holds a blazing sword aloft; below, to his right, is a pair of ferocious lions, one beast sinking its teeth into the head of the second. To his left is a cluster of four naked infants gazing upwards, seeking St Michael's protection.

Affixed to the front, a bronze tablet reads DURING THE GREAT WAR 1914 - 1919 THE NAMES WERE RECORDED ON THIS SITE OF 2130 MEN WHO FROM OFFICES IN THE PARISHES OF THIS UNITED BENEFICE VOLUNTEERED TO SERVE THEIR COUNTRY IN THE NAVY AND ARMY + OF THESE IT IS KNOWN THAT AT LEAST 170 GAVE THEIR LIVES FOR THE FREEDOM OF THE WORLD.

# LONDON EC3

## Victims of Oppression
ST BOTOLPH WITHOUT ALDGATE CHURCH, ALDGATE EC3

Unveiled in 1985 'Sanctuary' at St Botolph without Aldgate church, was designed by Naomi Blake. Born in Czechoslovakia she survived internment at Auschwitz concentration camp, and subsequently studied art at the Hornsey School of Art, London from 1955 – 1960.
The sculpture itself is a seated androgynous figure with its back against the rock of faith as if drawing courage and strength from it to get up and face life.

The plaque reads:
'SANCTUARY  BY NAOMI BLAKE  1985  TO ALL VICTIMS OF OPPRESSION'

# LONDON EC4

## National Firefighters Memorial
CARTER LANE GARDENS/PETER'S HILL EC4

The Memorial unveiled in 1991 is located on the south side of St. Paul's Cathedral which is symbolically portrayed as a famous and iconic building which stood in defiance of all of the fires burning and general destruction around it, caused by the Blitz on London.

The Memorial, depicting a Fire Officer and two Firemen, was originally called 'Blitz' and intended as a tribute to those men and women who fought against fire on the streets of London during the Blitz of World War II, when the city was struck by bombs on 57 consecutive nights in a sustained campaign of bombing. The north side of the plinth carries reliefs representing women working in the Fire Brigade in WW2. The memorial was re-dedicated in 2003 making it a national monument that would commemorate not just the firefighters who died in World War II, but the lives of all firefighters who were killed in the line of duty in the United Kingdom. The list of names is updated as necessary and the total number on the plinth is over 2250. Inscription - "[[BLITZ]] THE HEROES WITH GRIMY FACES IN HONOUR AND MEMORY OF THOSE FIREFIGHTERS WHO GAVE THEIR LIVES IN THE DEFENCE OF THE NATION 1939-1945 THIS MONUMENT WAS COMMISSIONED BY THE FOUNDER MASTER OF THE GUILD OF FIREFIGHTERS SUPPORTED BY PUBLIC AND SERVICE DONATIONS MCMXC SCULPTOR= JOHN W MILLS ARCA FRBS THE MEMORIAL WAS RE-DEDICATED THE UNITED KINGDOM FIREFIGHTERS NATIONAL MEMORIAL AND UNVEILLED BY THE ROYAL HIGHNESS THE PRINCESS ROYAL (PATRON OF THE FIREFIGHTERS MEMORIAL CHARITIES TRUST) 16 SEPTEMBER, 2003 THIS MEMORIAL WAS UNVEILED BY HER MAJESTY QUEEN ELIZABETH THE QUEEN MOTHER ON 4 MAY 1991

# LONDON EC4

## The National Submariners' War Memorial
VICTORIA EMBANKMENT EC4

GRADE: II* War memorial, unveiled 1922. Architect AH Ryan Tenison, bronze sculpture by Frederick Brook Hitch. Later additions for the Second World War unveiled in 1959. The inability to perform burials following losses at sea was a common part of the Naval experience and had led over previous years to the erection of a number of memorials to sailors of the Royal Navy, Merchant Marine, and other services such as the RNLI.

The First World War, however, was the first time in which submarines would play a significant military role. Britain had 57 operational submarines at the beginning of the war, with 15 under construction. Their most important function was the defence of Atlantic merchant shipping convoys against German U-boat attacks. At the war's end Britain had a fleet of 137 serving boats, with a further 78 under construction. Fifty-four boats were lost during the war and the lives of 138 officers and 1,225 men, approximately one-third of the Submarine Service's total personnel.

In 1959 new panels commemorating the Submarine Service's Second World War losses were unveiled.

The memorial consists of a monumental stepped granite pier carrying a large bronze plaque comprising a bas-relief underwater scene. The centerpiece of the bas-relief depicts the cross section of a submarine control room with the Captain to the fore beneath the periscope. Around the vessel is a host of mythical sea spirits or mermen tugging at the nets which are ensnaring it.

The cornice is crowned by an escutcheon resembling the Submarine Service 'Dolphin' badge; at each end are ships' prows clasped by putti. The base has a relief of a submarine cruising on the surface of the sea and the dates 1914 and 1918. The pilasters contain the lists of 50 submarines lost in the First World War and 82 in the Second World War; the capitals are embellished with the Royal Navy insignia and the bases with laurel wreaths.

The frieze has relief lettering reading ERECTED TO THE MEMORY OF THE OFFICERS AND MEN OF THE BRITISH NAVY WHO LOST THEIR LIVES SERVING IN SUBMARINES 1914-1918 AND 1939-1945.

Attached to the sides of the plaque are the allegorical female figures of Truth and Justice supported on miniature pedestals with dolphin consoles. Fixed to the wall to either side are 40 bronze wreath-hooks in the form of anchors, which are a distinctive feature of the memorial.

# LONDON N1

## Islington Green War Memorial
ISLINGTON MEMORIAL GREEN, UPPER STREET N1

The war memorial for Islington Green unveiled in 2006 was commissioned from the artist John Maine by the London Borough of Islington. The project formed part of the upgrading of the Green, and replaced a "temporary" memorial which had stood on the site since 1918.
Inscriptions on the ground either side of the ring: SEA AIR HOME LAND
On the ground in front of the ring, with a cross: IN MEMORY OF THE FALLEN
John Maine's work is sculpted from granite and recalls a memorial wreath on a grand scale. The circular motif is also intended to act as a sign of inclusiveness and to signal that the Green is a space for contemplation open to the whole community. The surrounding landscape design by J&L Gibbons complements the memorial.

## La Délivrance
REGENTS PARK ROAD N3 3JH

Grade: II* War statue, designed by Émile Guillaume, and unveiled in 1927.

'La Délivrance' is one of a number of casts of an allegorical statue by Émile Oscar Guillaume in memory of an early success in the First World War. The sculpture was inspired by the allied victory in the Battle of Marne, which took place in 1914 and in which French and British forces thwarted the German drive on Paris.

Eleven casts of La Délivrance were presented to the cities of France and Belgium which had been occupied or destroyed in the First World War.

The statue was exhibited at the 1920 Salon, where Guillaume won a medal. It was purchased by newspaper proprietor Viscount Rothermere, who presented it to Finchley Urban District Council due to his long association with the area.

The statue was unveiled in 1927 in front of a crowd of around 8,000. The statue is cast in bronze and stands on a pink polished granite pedestal. The figure is a female nude with upward stretched arms with a sword in her right hand. She stands on tiptoes upon a hemisphere which is mounted on a faceted drum pedestal and a square base. The hilt of the figure's sword and the front of the base of the statue are inscribed with the title of the piece. An information panel recounts: 'LA DELIVERANCE THIS STATUE BY EMILE GUILLAUME SYMBOLIZES THE EMOTION INSPIRED AMONG THE ALLIED NATIONS WHEN THE ARMIES OF BRITAIN AND FRANCE DEFEATED THE INVADING GERMAN ARMIES AT THE BATTLE OF THE MARNE SEPTEMBER 1914 PRESENTED BY VISCOUNT ROTHERMERE'.

### Boer War Memorial and Flanking Cannon
Corner of HIGHBURY PLACE AND HIGHBURY CRESCENT N5

GRADE: II 1905 By Bertram Mackennal. Plinth of granite, pedestal of Portland stone with bronze plaques, the cornice to the south loaded with emblems of war in bronze. The bronze statue above of a female figure representing glory. Female figure holds a small figure of victory in her right hand, laurel wreath in left hand. Draped standard, rifle, sword, helmet and laurel wreath at the base of the figure. The memorial is flanked by two small cast-iron cannon.
Inscription: "HOW SLEEP THE BRAVE WHO SINK TO REST BY ALL THEIR COUNTRY'S WISHES BLESS'D."
IN HONOUR OF NINETY-EIGHT ISLINGTONIANS WHO DIED FOR THEIR COUNTRY IN THE SOUTH AFRICAN WAR, 1899 - 1903.
ERECTED BY THEIR FELLOW-TOWNSMEN JULY 1905.

### Hornsey War Memorial Chapel    151 PARK ROAD N8 8JD

GRADE: II Opened in 1921 designed by George Lethbridge. A red brick and Portland stone chapel, the interior is wood panelled and the names of the fallen are carved into the panels organised by military unit. The memorial chapel was originally sited on the North Wing of Hornsey Central Hospital. The original hospital has been demolished and the Hornsey Central Health Centre erected in its place but the chapel maintained in its original location. Wreaths in stone above entrance to chapel. Hornsey Coat of Arms above external doorway.

Inscription outside: 1914 THE BOROUGH OF HORNSEY WAR MEMORIAL 1919

Inside frieze of walls is inscribed with painted inscriptions reading:
FAITHFUL UNTO DEATH (east),
STEADFAST AND UNDISMAYED THEY GAVE THEIR ALL (south),
THEIR NAME LIVETH FOR EVERMORE (west)
THEY DIED THAT YOU MIGHT LIVE IN PEACE AND HONOUR (north).

# LONDON N12

## Men Of Finchley WW1 And WW2
FINCHLEY UNITED SERVICES CLUB, 307 BALLARDS LANE N12 8LY

The Memorial remembers those servicemen and women up to the present day who have lost their lives in conflict. Finchley War Memorial is located outside the United Services Club. Unveiled in 1925 and attended by thousands of people. One thousand Men of Finchley, Husbands, Sons and Comrades made the Supreme Sacrifice in World War One in the hour of their Country's need.

The Bronze sculptured panel contains a carved relief with the figures of three servicemen a Soldier in full trench kit, with steel helmet, cape and fixed bayonet flanked by the busts of a Sailor and a Airman.

Inscription on main bronze panel: VICTORY WON BY SACRIFICE

Below the soldier: AT THE GOING DOWN OF THE SUN AND IN THE MORNING WE WILL REMEMBER THEM

Main inscription: IN GRATEFUL MEMORY OF MEN OF FINCHLEY WHO BY SERVICE ON LAND SEA AND IN THE AIR GAVE THEIR LIVES FOR THEIR COUNTRY 1914 - 1919  1939 - 1945

Metal gates: St. KILDA

Either side of the memorial are two memorial plaques the Finchley Metropolitan Tramway War Memorial (18 names), and the Hendon Garage War Memorial (52 names), who were relocated after the buildings where they were hanging were demolished.

# LONDON N22

## Wood Green War Memorial

HIGH ROAD N22

GRADE: II A Greek-inspired memorial screen, commemorating the 990 men of Wood Green who lost their lives in the First World War.
Portland stone with gold mosaic panels above, bronze inscription panels below; York stone steps. A tripartite screen with projecting central pedimental section and projecting wings.
The upper register, divided by Ionic pilasters sports round tablets with bay wreaths, listing Great War battle honours: Salonika, Mesopotamia, Egypt; Belgium, France, Italy, Gallipoli; Jutland, Heligoland, Falklands, Zeebrugge; and Palestine, India and Africa.
In the centre, a roundel with relief of ST George and the Dragon with the inscription ERECTED BY PUBLIC SUBSCRIPTION BY THE INHABITANTS OF WOOD GREEN 1920.
Along the frieze above is inscribed in Roman capitals 'GREATER LOVE HATH NO MAN THAN THIS THAT A MAN LAY DOWN HIS LIFE FOR HIS FRIENDS'.
The frieze at mid-height is inscribed 'AND IN MEMORY ALSO OF THOSE WHO GAVE THEIR LIVES 1939-1945'.
Central lower panel is inscribed 'TO THE UNDYING MEMORY OF THE MEN OF WOOD GREEN WHO GAVE THEIR LIVES IN THE GREAT WAR 1914-1918 1939-1945'.
The lower register is divided by fluted Doric pilasters, and sports six bronze tablets with the names of the dead.

# LONDON NW1

## London and North Western Railway War Memorial
EUSTON RAILWAY STATION,
EUSTON SQUARE,
EUSTON ROAD NW1

GRADE: II* 1921 War Memorial to commemorate the 3,719 LNWR employees who fell in the First World War. Designed by Reginald Wynn Owen, architect to the London & North Western Railway Company (LNWR). Bronze figures modelled by Ambrose Neale.

The memorial consists of a tall (13m high) obelisk of Portland stone on a tall pedestal, on a grey granite circular stepped base. The top of the obelisk is carved with four crosses in relief with bronze wreaths encircling their feet. Stepped buttresses at each angle of the pedestal support four over life-sized bronze statues representing the Navy, the Infantry, the Artillery and the Air Force, resting on reversed arms, with heads bowed. The front face of the obelisk is inscribed IN MEMORY OF OUR GLORIOUS DEAD.

Inscription on granite panel: IN GRATEFUL MEMORY OF 3719 MEN OF THE LONDON AND NORTH-WESTERN RAILWAY COMPANY WHO FOR THEIR COUNTRY, JUSTICE AND FREEDOM SERVED AND DIED IN THE GREAT WAR 1914-1919 THIS MONUMENT WAS RAISED BY THEIR COMRADES AND THE COMPANY AS A LASTING MEMORIAL TO THEIR DEVOTION.

Stone inscription panels on the east and west sides commemorate employees of the London Midland and Scottish Railway Company (into which the LNWR was absorbed in 1921) who died in the Second World War REMEMBER THE MEN AND WOMEN OF THE LONDON MIDLAND AND SCOTTISH 1939 RAILWAY 1945.

# LONDON NW2

## Prisoners of War and Victims of Concentration Camps 1914–1945 Memorial
GLADSTONE PARK, DOLLIS HILL LANE NW2 6JA

Grade: II Memorial sculpture group. By Fred Kormis unveiled in 1969. A powerful and moving sculptural group, exploring changing inner states through a spatial sequence of figures. A rare example of a memorial to prisoners of war and concentration camp victims, deriving poignancy from Kormis' own experiences in a Siberian prisoner of war camp. In 1967 Kormis recalled his own experiences as a prisoner of war: 'First there is the numb shock of realizing you are a prisoner in the hands of the enemy. Then there is the dawning awareness of your predicament and the primitive conditions. The next phase is the thought of escape and freedom. After that many succumb to despair and a sense of hopelessness. Others overcome their dejection and manage to escape'. This group comprises five fibreglass resin sculptures with bronze powder. Four male seated figures occupy a series of stepped platforms, with a fifth standing at the margin of the group. The group is set against a sloping wall of shuttered reinforced concrete, painted white. A plaque reads 'TO THE MEMORY OF PRISONERS OF WAR AND VICTIMS OF CONCENTRATION CAMPS 1914–1945'. Although the seated figures are arranged in contrasting postures they depict male figures of similar appearance, with swaddling-like wound strips of clothing, as if the same individual is shown at different states or conditions. Kormis described the sequence of figures as 'a five-chapter novel, each chapter describing a successive state of mind of internment: stupor after going into captivity; longing for freedom; fighting against gloom; hope lost; and hope again.'

# International Brigade Spanish Civil War Memorial
JUBILEE GARDENS
BELVEDERE ROAD SE1

National memorial and sculpture by Ian Walters to the 526 killed in Spanish Civil War who went to Spain from Britain and Ireland. Unveiled in 1985. Moved to new site in the park in April 2012.

Sculpted abstract group. Four figures support a wounded, kneeling figure, their free arms out-stretched. Two of the figures have open palms in the act of fending off to protect, and two have their fists clenched, expressing defiant resistance. Sculpture is mounted on black stone plinth. Inscription in gilt incised lettering.

Inscription front face:
INTERNATIONAL BRIGADE IN HONOUR OF OVER 2100 MEN & WOMEN VOLUNTEERS WHO LEFT THESE SHORES TO FIGHT SIDE BY SIDE WITH THE SPANISH PEOPLE IN THEIR HEROIC STRUGGLE AGAINST FASCISM 1939-1939. MANY WERE WOUNDED AND MAIMED, 526 WERE KILLED THEIR EXAMPLE INSPIRED THE WORLD

Inscription 3 o'clock face: "THEY WENT BECAUSE THEIR OPEN EYES COULD SEE NO OTHER WAY"

Inscription 9 o'clock face: "YET FREEDOM! YET THY BANNER, TORN, BUT FLYING, STREAMS LIKE THE THUNDER-STORM AGAINST THE WIND"

Back face: THIS MEMORIAL UNVEILED BY MICHAEL FOOT 5TH OCTOBER 1985 WAS MADE POSSIBLE BY THE SUPPORT OF MANY DEMOCRATIC ORGANISATIONS INDIVIDUALS AND THE GREATER LONDON COUNCIL.

# LONDON SE1

## The St Saviours Southwark War Memorial
### 97 BOROUGH HIGH STREET SE1

GRADE: II War memorial. Unveiled 1922. Modelled and sculpted by Captain Philip Lindsay Clark DSO and representing an advancing infantryman in battledress with bayonet fixed rifle on shoulder. Tall plinth with bronze reliefs representing aerial and naval combat. To the front a depiction of St George and the Dragon; to the rear, facing the City, an allegorical representation of a mourning woman, Grief, with a babe clasping a dove.

Inscription GIVE HONOUR TO THE MEN OF ST SAVIOURS SOUTHWARK WHO GAVE THEIR LIVES FOR THE EMPIRE 1914-1918. THEIR NAMES ARE INSCRIBED WITHIN THE PARISH CHURCH. MAY THEIR MEMORY LIVE FOR EVER IN THE MINDS OF MEN.

West face: THIS MEMORIAL WAS ERECTED BY THE PARISHIONERS OF ST SAVIOURS SOUTHWARK IN THE YEAR 1922.

# Soviet War Memorial
GERALDINE MARY
HARMSWORTH PARK
LAMBETH ROAD  SE1

---

The memorial commemorates the sacrifice of 27 million lives by the citizens and armed forces of the former Soviet Union in its joint struggle with the United Kingdom, the United States and France to defeat fascism during World War II. It is the only monument of its kind in the UK.
Bronze structure comprising functioning bell held aloft by a bowed figure. Bell and figure set on raised stone step. Bell structure stands at one end of paved area. At opposite end of paved area is a flat marble tablet.
Inscription
(FIRST LINE OF INSCRIPTION IN RUSSIAN)
THIS MEMORIAL COMMEMORATES THE 27 MILLION SOVIET CITIZENS & SERVICE MEN & WOMEN WHO DIED FOR THE ALLIED VICTORY IN WWII THIS MEMORIAL WAS RAISED BY PUBLIC SUBSCRIPTION IN GREAT BRITAIN AND RUSSIA (REPEATED IN RUSSIAN) WE SHALL REMEMBER THEM

Unveiled on 9 May 1999 by the Secretary of State for Defence George Robertson, and the Russian ambassador Yuri Fokine. The date of the unveiling was significant as 9 May is marked as Victory Day in Russia. Since its inauguration the memorial has been the site of commemorations of Victory Day, Holocaust Memorial Day and Remembrance Sunday.
The memorial was designed by Russian sculptor Sergei Shcherbakov. The granite memorial tablet was made by British stonemason Gary Breeze.

# LONDON SE1

## Victory Arch Waterloo Railway Station

WATERLOO ROAD SE1

GRADE: II Built 1919-22. Entrance arch to Waterloo Station commemorates the London and South Western and the Southern Railway men who gave their lives in the First and Second World Wars. Waterloo is UK's largest station, covering an area of 24.5 acres.

Above the arch is Britannia holding the torch of liberty with figures either side. To the left of the arch above the date 1914 is the figure of Bellona, goddess of war, surrounded by four mourning figures. To the right above the date 1918 is the seated figure of Peace surrounded by five figures, including an infant. Peace is holding a small winged figure of Victory.
Inscription around the arch just above the clock:
DEDICATED TO THE EMPLOYEES OF THE COMPANY WHO FELL IN THE WAR.
Seven cartouches with names of campaigns: BELGIUM; ITALY; DARDANELLES; FRANCE; MESOPOTAMIA; EGYPT; NORTH SEA
Plaques under the arch bear the names of 585 LSWR employees who lost their lives in WWI.
Inscription: 1914 ROLL OF HONOUR 1918
NAMES OF THE COMPANY'S EMPLOYEES WHO GAVE THEIR LIVES IN THE GREAT WAR

The special significance of the monument within the post-First World War genre is that the LSWR staff themselves were, uniquely, consulted on its design.

# Violette Szabo & SOE The Special Operations Executive
ALBERT EMBANKMENT SE1

Violette Szabo was among the 117 SOE agents who did not survive their missions to France. Sculpture by Karen Newman, unveiled 2009.

Inscription on the front of the plinth: S. O. E. The Special Operations Executive was secretly formed for the purpose of recruiting agents, men and women of many nationalities, who would volunteer to continue the fight for freedom, by performing acts of sabotage in countries occupied by the enemy during the Second World War. This monument is in honour of all the courageous S.O.E. Agents: those who did survive and those who did not survive their perilous missions. Their services were beyond the call of duty. In the pages of history their names are carved with pride.

On the southern face of the plaque: The Maquis - French Resistance Fighters  470 SOE agents were sent on sabotage missions to occupied France where they fought with networks of French resistance fighters who played an important part in the liberation of France in 1944.

On the northern face of the plinth: The Heroes of Telemark.  In 1943 Norwegian resistance commandos sponsored by the SOE raided the enemy occupied Norsk hydro plant in the Telemark region of Norway. This successful raid sabotaged the machinery that was producing heavy water which is used in the manufacture of the atomic bomb. Thanks to those heroic Norwegian commandos the enemy's attempt to develop the atomic bomb was thwarted.

LONDON SE1

# LONDON SE11

## Following the Leader (Memorial to the Children Killed in the Blitz)
DARLEY HOUSE,
VAUXHALL GARDENS ESTATE,
LAUD STREET SE11

---

GRADE: II Sculptural relief in coloured concrete. 1949 by Peter Laszlo Peri. Mounted on the stair tower of Darley House.

An early example of the naturalistic social art of this Hungarian Jewish émigré artist and a rare example of LCC post-war public art in the context of social housing, commemorating children killed in the Blitz.

This area was extensively bombed, and most of the houses that survived were taken down when peace broke out. Darley House was built in the late 1940s.

The memorial depicts a naturalistic group of six children, holding hands in a spiral towards the sky. The group spring from a narrow two-stage concrete plinth. The relief is of red ochre coloured concrete laid over an expanded metal mesh and is 4.73m tall and 1.65m wide. Peri had developed a technique for sculpting in wet concrete directly to a wall. He would secure an armature of wire mesh to the wall and trowel coloured concrete on. The technique attracted interest from industry and an exhibition of his work in 1938 had been sponsored by the Cement and Concrete Association.

# LONDON SE16

**22nd Battalion, The London Regiment (The Queen's) Memorial**     OLD JAMAICA ROAD SE16

GRADE: II Memorial unveiled in 1921 honours the officers and soldiers of the Territorial battalion: 22nd Battalion The London Regiment (The Queen's), who lost their lives in World War I. Most of the men were from the old Bermondsey Borough. The war memorial is a permanent testament to the sacrifice made by this battalion in the World War I, it is of historic and cultural significance both at a local and a national level. The memorial commemorates the role of a Territorial unit in World War I; the first time that part-time volunteers, with civilian occupations, served en masse in a war abroad.

Following the end of World War II, a plaque was added to the memorial to commemorate the dead of the 6th (Bermondsey) Battalion of the Queen's Royal Regiment (as the battalion was by this time known).

Built of Portland stone blocks, the memorial is in the form of a wall, set back from the edge of the pavement, and to either side flanking walls advance to the pavement edge.
Inscription: 22nd BATTN LONDON REGT 1914-1918. Above the inscription is a carved relief of the regimental crest; the Paschal lamb over a banner reading THE QUEEN'S, and beneath is the Roll of Honour carved into the face of the stone. The ends of the flanking walls bear Latin inscriptions with English translations beneath. These read: BE THOU MINDFUL OF THE COURAGE OF HIM THAT IS FALLEN and FOR HIS VERY ASHES DO CRY OUT IN TRIUMPH. To the inside of the flanking walls is a list of campaigns and battles in which the battalion fought, including the ten for which they were awarded battle honours.

# LONDON SW1

## Australian War Memorial

HYDE PARK CORNER SW1

This memorial unveiled in 2003 commemorates the Australian service men and women who served in WWI and WWII.

The memorial comprises a semicircular curved wall of grey-green granite slabs, cut in Australia before being shipped to London. The granite stones are inscribed with the names of 23,844 towns in which the Australian soldiers were born in Australia and elsewhere. Parts of some town names are picked out in bolder type, creating the names of 47 battles in which Australia was involved. In the summer months, water runs down over the names, intended to evoke "memories of service, suffering and sacrifice". The curved wall is set facing a downwards slope of grass, forming an amphitheatre.

The use of green/grey Australian granite reflects the essence of the bush. Principal architect Peter Tonkin explains that 'the form chosen for the memorial reflects the sweep of Australian landscape, the breadth and generosity of our people, the openness that we believe should characterise our culture'. Also reflected in the shape of the wall are echoes of Australia's unique flora and cultural heritage – the gumleaf and the boomerang.

Four blocks bear the crest of Australia and the insignia of the three branches of the Australian armed services, and the dedicatory inscription:
"WHATEVER BURDEN YOU ARE TO CARRY WE ALSO WILL SHOULDER THAT BURDEN"
"Australia–United Kingdom 1914–1918   1939 – 1945". One of the stones in front of the monument has a map of the world with labels identifying the places where Australians fought. The others read:
"Australian War Memorial dedicated in the presence of Her Majesty the Queen, the Hon John Howard MP Prime Minister of Australia, the Rt Hon Tony Blair MP Prime Minister of the United Kingdom and contingents of Australian and British veterans, 11 November 2003."
"Tonkin Zulaikha Greer - Architects Janet Laurence - Artist"

## Bali Bombings Memorial

HORSE GUARDS ROAD  SW1

A memorial by Martin Cook and Gary Breeze to victims of the 2002 bombings in Bali, Indonesia. It was unveiled on 12 October 2006, the fourth anniversary of the bombings. The memorial commemorates the victims of all nationalities, with those from Britain listed apart at the centre of the inscription. Standing near the wall is a granite globe with 202 doves carved across its surface. Martin Cook explained its symbolism: "All of the 202 doves are unique, to represent each life lost and as symbols for peace. The globe shows how the victims came from all parts of the world and how indiscriminate terrorism is".

On the ground surrounding the sphere: YOU WERE ROBBED OF LIFE. YOUR SPIRIT ENRICHES OURS. Inscribed into the stone wall: IN MEMORY OF THE 202 INNOCENT PEOPLE KILLED BY AN ACT OF TERRORISM IN KUTA ON THE ISLAND OF BALI, INDONESIA ON THE 12th OCTOBER 2002. THE BRITISH CITIZENS LOST HERE ARE LOVINGLY REMEMBERED  Under this is a list of 28 names, followed by their age. The panels either side list the other 174 people who died from Australia, Indonesia, Germany, Switzerland, Portugal, Italy, Poland, Greece, the US and Japan.

The 2002 Bali Bombings terrorist attack involved the detonation of three bombs - a suicide bomb in Paddy's Bar, another, more powerful car bomb exploded in front of the Sari Club, a third bomb was detonated in front of the U.S. consulate on the island of Bali.

A week later, Indonesian police arrested more than 30 terrorists suspected of planning and executing the bombings. The investigations that followed the terrorist attack identified the terrorist organization Jemaah Islamiyah (an Islamic group) as responsible for the bombings.

# LONDON SW1

## Battle of Britain Monument

VICTORIA EMBANKMENT SW1

The Battle of Britain monument unveiled in 2005. Sculptor Paul Day. The core of the monument is a number of scenes, not just of the Battle of Britain itself, but also related topics of both military and ordinary life at that time. The scenes depict workers who were supporting the airmen in the Battle: the spotters looking for enemy planes, the ground technical staff, women working in munitions factories along with people in the blitz.

Inscription - WAR WITH NAZI GERMANY BEGAN IN SEPTEMBER 1939 AND BY JUNE 1940 HITLER'S FORCES HAD OCCUPIED MOST OF WESTERN EUROPE, WITH FASCIST REGIMES ALSO RULING IN ITALY AND SPAIN. FURTHER EXPANSION OF NAZI DOMINATION IN EUROPE DEPENDED ON BRITAIN BEING NEUTRALISED BY EITHER INVASION OR SURRENDER UNDER GERMAN TERMS. AS PRIME MINISTER WINSTON CHURCHILL VOWED THAT BRITAIN WOULD NEVER SURRENDER, THE GERMAN HIGH COMMAND COMMENCED 'OPERATION SEALION', THE INVASION OF BRITAIN. THE FIRST PRIORITY WAS FOR GERMANY'S LUFTWAFFE TO GAIN CONTROL OF THE SKIES ABOVE THE ENGLISH CHANNEL AND SOUTH EAST ENGLAND TO PREVENT THE ROYAL NAVY AND ROYAL AIR FORCE ATTACKING THE GERMAN INVASION FORCES WHILE THEY WERE AT SEA. ON 10TH JULY 1940 THE LUFTWAFFE STARTED A SERIES OF ATTACKS ON PORTS AND CONVOYS IN THE ENGLISH CHANNEL. USING ADVANCED WARNING FROM RADAR STATIONS. BRITAIN WAS DEFENDED IN THE AIR BY RAF FIGHTER COMMAND UNDER AIR CHIEF MARSHAL HUGH DOWDING, WITH BACKUP FROM BALLOON BARRAGES AND ANTI-AIRCRAFT GUN INSTALLATIONS ON THE GROUND. BY EARLY AUGUST, WITH GERMAN INVASION FORCES AND LANDING CRAFT BEING ASSEMBLED ON THE FRENCH COAST, THE ATTACKS BECAME MUCH HEAVIER, WITH GERMAN BOMBERS AND FIGHTERS CONCENTRATING ON RAF AIRFIELDS AND AIRCRAFT FACTORIES. DURING THE HOT SUMMER OF 1940, PILOTS, MANY UNDER TWENTY

# THE BATTLE OF BRITAIN

YEARS OF AGE. WOULD 'SCRAMBLE' FOR THEIR AIRCRAFT TO INTERCEPT ENEMY RAIDS AS OFTEN AS FIVE TIMES A DAY AND INTO THE NIGHT. OUTNUMBERED IN AIR BATTLES, EXHAUSTED RAF SQUADRONS WERE ROTATED TO STATIONS ELSEWHERE IN BRITAIN AND REPLACED BY FRESH UNITS, OFTEN CONTAINING A HIGH PROPORTION OF LESS EXPERIENCED PILOTS. BY EARLY SEPTEMBER THE INCREASINGLY CRITICAL SITUATION, ESPECIALLY IN AIR VICE MARSHAL KEITH PARK'S 11 GROUP, WAS RELIEVED TEMPORARILY BY THE LUFTWAFFE TURNING ITS ATTENTION TO LONDON IN A FINAL ATTEMPT TO BREAK THE BRITISH WILL TO RESIST. THE TURNING POINT CAME ON 15TH SEPTEMBER WHEN TWO HUGE AIR ATTACKS WERE REPULSED WITH HEAVY LOSSES LEADING HITLER TO CONCEDE THAT AN INVASION WOULD FAIL. DAY AND NIGHT ATTACKS CONTINUED THROUGH TO MAY 1941 BUT THE MAIN ASSAULT HAD ENDED BY LATE OCTOBER 1940. THIS FAILURE TO SUBDUE BRITAIN WOULD ULTIMATELY COST GERMANY THE WAR. OF THE 2936 PILOTS AND AIRCREW WHO FOUGHT IN RAF FIGHTER COMMAND IN THE BATTLE OF BRITAIN, 544 LOST THEIR LIVES AND A FURTHER 795 DID NOT LIVE TO SEE THE FINAL VICTORY IN 1945. ONE IN SIX WERE FROM COUNTRIES OUTSIDE THE UNITED KINGDOM AND ON THE PLAQUES SURROUNDING THIS MONUMENT, THEIR NAMES HAVE BEEN GROUPED ACCORDING TO COUNTRY OF ORIGIN. THE PLAQUES ALSO FEATURE THE BADGES OF THEIR SQUADRONS. IT IS IN HONOUR OF THE SPIRIT AND SACRIFICE OF THOSE KNOWN AS 'THE FEW' AND THOSE SUPPORTING THEM THAT THIS MONUMENT HAS BEEN ERECTED.

*Panel above:* First Panel – Fighter Command
a – Pilots at rest   Waiting for the signal to be brought to readiness or to scramble allowed the pilots much needed time to rest.
b – The observers   Scattered around the coast and inland, the 30,000 strong Observer Corps ceaselessly scoured the air to intercept, visually and orally, enemy raiders.
c – Mechanics and Riggers   None praise the work of the ground crews more highly than the pilots themselves, whose very lives depended on the vigilance and efficiency of their RAF colleagues.
d – Scramble   The centre piece of the monument is "Scramble", the airmen running towards their planes having been ordered to scramble to intercept enemy planes. It is the very symbol of the Battle. In this case, the pilots surge off the wall, out of their picture and onto the pavement, into our world, a reminder to say that these men really did exist.
e – Large pilot's head & plotters
f – Tales from the Mess   Young, inexperienced pilots drank in the commentaries of their battle hardy counterparts.

*Panel below:* Second Panel – Britain at War
g – The Slit Trench   Kentish hop pickers watching from the shelter of slit trenches the air battle raging overhead.
h – Gunners   The threat appears in the form of aerial bombardment.
i – Woman Power   Women worked in aircraft and munitions factories and flew the aircraft from the factory to the airfield.
j – Dogfight   The head of a Messerschmitt pilot on the shoulder of an RAF one creates the sense of a dual being fought out by two knights of the air.
k – St Paul's   St Paul's became the symbol of resistance during the Blitz having remained standing while all around was demolished.
l – Searching the Ruins   One of the most troubling aspects of the Battle was the bombing of heavily populated areas. This scene is in homage to the rescue services.
m – Brew Up   Making tea in an Anderson shelter.

# LONDON SW1

## Boadicea (Boudicca) Statuary Group

VICTORIA EMBANKMENT SW1

GRADE: II 1850s sculpture by Thomas Thornycroft. Larger than life-sized bronze statue depicts chariot drawn by two rearing horses. Boudicca stands in the centre of the chariot holding a spear in one hand and with her other arm oustretched. Her two daughters stand either side of her in the chariot.

The statue stands on a grey granite plinth.

Inscription - BOADICEA (BOUDICCA) QUEEN OF THE ICENI WHO DIED A.D. 61 AFTER LEADING HER PEOPLE AGAINST THE ROMAN INVADER.

On the right side text from William Cowper's poem Boadicea, (1782): REGIONS CAESAR NEVER KNEW THY POSTERITY SHALL SWAY. The left side reads, THIS STATUE BY THOMAS THORNYCROFT WAS PRESENTED TO LONDON BY HIS SON SIR JOHN ISAAC THORNYCROFT C.E. AND PLACED HERE BY THE LONDON COUNTY COUNCIL A.D. 1902

Boadicea led the British Iceni tribe in revolt against the Romans. It has been estimated that over 70,000 people were killed in the towns of Colchester, St Albans and London by the rebel forces.

Boudica was queen of the Iceni during the early Roman occupation of Britain. However when her husband Prasutagus died and left half of his property and lands to their two daughters, and the other half to Rome, the Romans took control of all the land and possessions. They publicly flogged Boudica and dishonoured her daughters, inciting her to rebellion and vengeance. Her people, who had previously been allies of the Romans, were also badly treated and joined forces with other Celtic tribes under her leadership.

She led them to victory on three occasions, in Colchester, London and St. Albans. But, despite overwhelming numbers, the Britons lost the crucial Battle of Watling Street to the Romans. After the battle, the remaining Iceni dispersed or were captured and taken into slavery. As a result of the defeat, the Romans occupied Britain for over 350 years.

# LONDON SW1

## Cadiz Memorial
HORSE GUARDS PARADE SW1

GRADE: II Memorial. 1814 Cast iron and bronze. Remarkable exotic design comprising a genuine French mortar mounted on a dramatic Chinese dragon, set on a "rustic" cast pedestal with inscription panels and Prince of Wales feather. Set up to commemorate the lifting of the French siege of Cadiz following Wellington's victory at Salamanca in 1812.

The text on the plinth on the north side is in Latin and the south side in English:
TO COMMEMORATE THE RAISING OF THE SIEGE OF CADIZ IN CONSEQUENCE OF THE GLORIOUS VICTORY GAINED BY THE DUKE OF WELLINGTON XXII JULY MDCCCXM THIS MORTAR CAST FOR THE DESTRUCTION OF THAT GREAT PORT, WITH POWERS SURPASSING ALL OTHERS AND ABANDONED BY THE BESIEGERS ON THEIR RETREAT WAS PRESENTED AS A TOKEN OF RESPECT AND GRATITUDE BY THE SPANISH NATION TO HIS ROYAL HIGHNESS THE PRINCE REGENT.

On their withdrawal the French deliberately destroyed their cannons. The Spanish must have retrieved and restored this mortar before presenting it, in gratitude, to the Prince Regent.

# LONDON SW1

## Canada Memorial

GREEN PARK SW1

On an information panel next to the memorial: Designed by Canadian sculptor Pierre Granche and unveiled by Her Majesty The Queen in 1994, this memorial pays tribute to the nearly one million Canadian and Newfoundland men and women who came to the United Kingdom to serve during the First and Second World Wars. In particular, it honours more than 100,000 brave Canadians and Newfoundlanders who made the ultimate sacrifice for peace and freedom.

The monument made of polished red granite from the Canadian shield, is inset with bronze maple leaves arranged in a windswept pattern. Set at an incline, shimmering water flows over the monument creating the impression of maple leaves floating down a stream. In a reversal of the autumnal process, the leaves continue to gradually change from a deep brown to a bright green, the colour of spring, of youth and regeneration.

The monument is divided into two sections representing Canadian and British participation in the two world wars. The compass rose in the middle orients the sculpture towards Halifax, Nova Scotia, the port from which most Canadians left for active service.

On the ground there is a compass, with inscription:
IN TWO WORLD WARS ONE MILLION CANADIANS CAME TO BRITAIN AND JOINED THE FIGHT FOR FREEDOM. FROM DANGER SHARED OUR FRIENDSHIP PROSPERS.

Around the brass outer edge of the compass circle: This monument was made possible by the generosity of ordinary people in Canada and Britain and in particular Canadian veterans of both World Wars who donated willingly for the cause.

The bronze leaves embedded in the granite are maple, the national symbol of Canada.

# LONDON SW1

## The Cenotaph
### WHITEHALL SW1

GRADE I The principal national memorial to the dead of Britain and the British Empire in the First World War and subsequent conflicts of the C20. The Portland stone memorial by Sir Edwin Lutyens, was unveiled by King George V on Armistice Day – 11 November 1920.

It is the focal point of the annual Remembrance Day commemorations. One of the most universally admired memorials in the world, embodying the profound grief caused by the tragic losses of the First World War and subsequent conflicts. Its austere and restrained design has been readily responded to by thousands in search of a place to lay tributes in memory of the absent dead. The word cenotaph derives from the Greek for an empty tomb. When first erected, the Cenotaph immediately caught the public imagination. This substitute for a tomb became taken up by huge numbers of mourners: over 1.25million came to pay their respects in the first week. At the top is a plain tomb chest on which lies a large laurel wreath. It stands on a three-staged base, which in turn stands on a tall shaft, set back towards its upper section. Beneath is the two-stage base. The dates for the World Wars are inscribed in Roman numerals on the base level above the shaft. On either end of the shaft, are carved stone bosses with laurels suspended by stone fillets. The only words on the memorial are inscribed on the north and south sides: THE GLORIOUS DEAD. Three flags, for each of the Armed Services are installed on each side of the base. The tapering of the design is minutely calculated, so that the vertical lines would, if continued, converge on a point 1000ft in the air, while the horizontal lines are fractionally curved, and would share a radial point 900ft below the pavement.

# LONDON SW1

## Chindit Memorial
VICTORIA EMBANKMENT GARDENS SW1

The Chindits were the largest of the allied Special Forces of the 2nd World War. They were formed and lead by Major General Orde Wingate DSO. The Chindits operated deep behind enemy lines in North Burma in the War against Japan. For many months they lived in and fought the enemy in the jungles of Japanese occupied Burma, totally relying on airdrops for their supplies. There were two Chindits expeditions into Burma, the first in 1943 consisted of a force of 3,000 men who marched over 1,000 miles during the campaign. The second expedition, in 1944 was on a much larger scale. It was the second largest airborne invasion of the war and consisted of a force of 20,000 British and Commonwealth soldiers.

The memorial was unveiled in 1990. Inscription:
THE CHINDIT BADGE PORTRAYING A CHINTHE, A MYTHICAL BEAST, GUARDIAN OF BURMESE TEMPLES FROM WHICH WAS DERIVED THE NAME CHINDITS, THEIR MOTTO BEING "THE BOLDEST MEASURES ARE THE SAFEST" IN MEMORY OF ALL WHO FOUGHT ON THE FIRST AND SECOND EXPEDITIONS INTO NORTH BURMA 1943 AND 1944 WITH THE CHINDIT SPECIAL FORCES".
FORMED TRAINED AND COMMANDED BY MAJOR GENERAL ORDE CHARLES WINGATE.DSO
CHINDITS CAME FROM THE ARMED FORCES OF THE UNITED KINGDOM, BURMA, HONG KONG, INDIA, NEPAL, WEST AFRICA AND THE UNITED STATES OF AMERICA.
AIR SUPPLY AND DIRECT OPERATIONAL SUPPORT WAS GIVEN BY THE ROYAL AIR FORCE AND 1ST AIR COMMANDO GROUP, UNITED STATES ARMY AIR FORCE AND 10TH UNITED STATES ARMY AIR FORCE.
VICTORY WAS HASTENED BY THE CHINDITS' DARING EXPLOITS BEHIND ENEMY LINES

The units involved are listed on the sides of the monument, as well as the names of four men of the Chindits who were awarded the Victoria Cross. The rear of the monument is dedicated to Wingate, with a plaque depicting his portrait.

# LONDON SW1

## Combined Forces Memorial

THE CLOISTERS, BROAD SANCTUARY SW1

In the west cloister of Westminster Abbey is a monument commemorating officers and men of the Submarine Service of the Royal Navy, the Commandos, and all ranks of the Airborne Forces and Special Air Service.
It was designed by the sculptor Gilbert Ledward, with three bronze figures in stone niches, with the dates 1939 and 1945 on tablets between. The models for the figures were serving members of the forces. The memorial was unveiled in 1948.
Beneath the sailor is a bronze plaque with two naval badges and the inscriptions: "To the Glory of God and in memory of the officers and men of the Submarine branch of the Royal Navy who have given their lives both in peace and war".
"The last enemy that shall be destroyed is death".
Beneath the soldier are two badges and the inscriptions:
"To the Glory of God and in memory of all ranks of the Commandos who fell in the Second World War 1939-1945".
"They performed whatsoever the King commanded".
Beneath the airman are two badges and the inscriptions:
"To the Glory of God and in memory of all ranks of the Airborne Forces and Special Air Service who fell in the Second World War 1939-1945".
"These were mighty men of valour".

## Armed Forces memorial

THE CLOISTERS, BROAD SANCTUARY SW1

In the south cloister is a memorial to members of the United Kingdom Armed Forces, both regular and reserve, who have lost their lives in conflicts since the end of the 1939-1945 war. It also remembers those of the Royal Fleet Auxiliary and the Merchant Navy. The memorial was unveiled in 2008 the sculptor was Tom Phillips, R.A. The centre text is in welded steel, with a brown covering made from earth gathered world wide from battle sites from different eras ie. from Battle, site of the battle of Hastings in 1066, Agincourt and the Somme. The fifteen samples were mixed and ground together to make a pigment bound in acrylic resin. Cut into the stonework around this, repeated four times, is the motto of the Armed Forces Memorial Appeal: REMEMBER THEM. TODAY. TOMORROW. FOREVER.

# LONDON SW1

## Commonwealth Memorial Gates  CONSTITUTION HILL SW1

The Commonwealth Memorial Gates unveiled in 2002. The main inscription reads: IN MEMORY OF THE FIVE MILLION VOLUNTEERS FROM THE INDIAN SUB-CONTINENT, AFRICA AND THE CARRIBEAN WHO FOUGHT WITH BRITAIN IN THE TWO WORLD WARS. Followed by the words of the Nigerian author and poet Ben Okri: "OUR FUTURE IS GREATER THAN OUR PAST." The names of holders of Victoria and George Crosses are engraved inside of the domed pavilion. Four stone pylons are carved with the names: India, Pakistan, Sri Lanka, Bangladesh, Africa, Caribbean, Kingdom of Nepal. They are topped by a bronze urn and gas flames, which are lit on such occasions as Remembrance Sunday, Armistice Day and Commonwealth Day.

On the information panel: A debt of honour - The Memorial Gates. With so many descendants of these volunteers now living in the United Kingdom, the Memorial Gates serve to remind us all of our shared sacrifices in times of greatest need.

**First World War** 1914 – 18. *Indian Sub-continent and the Kingdom of Nepal* - 1,440,500 men and women, including 100,000 Gurkhas, volunteered for military service in the Indian Army. They fought on the Western Front, in Gallipoli, Persia, Egypt, Palestine and Mesopotamia. *Africa* – the old British African colonies provided 62,000 troops and transport auxiliaries who fought in Africa. *Caribbean* – over 15,000 men served in the British West Indies Regiment and saw action in France Palestine, Egypt and Italy.

**Second World War** 1939 – 45 *Indian Sub-Continent and the Kingdom of Nepal* – over 2,500,000 including 132,000 Gurkhas, served in Burma, Malaya, Hong Kong, North and East Africa, France, Italy, Greece and throughout the Middle East. *Africa* – over 372,000, mostly from East and West Africa, served in the Middle East, East Africa, Italy and Burma. *Caribbean* – over 7,000 men and women volunteered to aid the war effort, many of whom saw action in the Middle East, Far East, East Africa and Italy.

# LONDON SW1

## Crimea and Indian Mutiny Memorial
BROAD SANCTUARY SW1

GRADE: II Memorial, 1859-61 by Sir George Gilbert Scott. Polished red granite column with Portland stone base dressing and sculpture. The column rises from a base with 4 lions and has a shaft-ring from which hang shields, a large Gothic capital surmounted by a lattern-cross and, over all, a statue of St. George and the dragon carved by J.R. Clayton, with statues of St Edward the Confessor, Henry III, Elizabeth I and Queen Victoria, carved by J. Birnie Philip. Erected in memory of the fallen of Westminster School who died in the Crimean War 1854-1856 and the Indian Mutiny 1857-1858. Inscription: TO THE MEMORY OF THOSE EDUCATED AT WESTMINSTER SCHOOL WHO DIED IN THE RUSSIAN AND INDIAN WARS A.D. 1854-1859 ON THE FIELD OF BATTLE OR FROM WOUNDS OR SICKNESS SOME IN EARLY YOUTH SOME FULL OF YEARS AND HONOURS BUT WHO ALL ALIKE GAVE THEIR LIVES FOR THEIR COUNTRY THIS COLUMN WAS ERECTED BY THEIR OLD SCHOOLFELLOWS IN TOKEN OF SORROW FOR THEIR LOSS OF PRIDE IN THEIR VALOUR AND IN FULL ASSURANCE THAT THE REMEMBRANCE OF THEIR HEROISM IN LIFE AND DEATH WILL INSPIRE THEIR SUCCESSORS AT WESTMINSTER WITH THE SAME COURAGE AND SELF-DEVOTION.

# LONDON SW1

## Fleet Air Arm Memorial
VICTORIA EMBANKMENT GARDENS SW1

The Fleet Air Arm Memorial, unveiled in June 2000 commemorates the service of the Royal Naval Air Service and the Fleet Air Arm in the First World War, the Second World War, the Korean War, the Falklands War and the Gulf War, including over 6,000 killed in all conflicts. The Fleet Air Arm is the operational group of the Royal Navy, responsible for the operation of the aircraft on board their ships, as well as search and rescue.

The memorial comprises a thin stone column on which stands a bronze statue of a naval airman, wearing a flying suit and helmet, and with wings attached to his arms resembling a winged victory or an angel. This bronze figure represents Daedalus from Ancient Greek mythology, who crafted wings from wax and feathers for himself and his son Icarus to escape Crete. But Icarus flew so close to the sun that the wax melted and he fell into the sea. Daedalus survived to mourn the fallen.

Inscription lower plinth, outer side:
FLEET AIR ARM

Inscription on lower plinth, inner side:
TO THE EVERLASTING MEMORY OF ALL THE MEN AND WOMEN FROM THE UNITED KINGDOM, THE BRITISH COMMONWEALTH AND THE MANY ALLIED NATIONS WHO HAVE GIVEN THEIR LIVES WHILST SERVING IN THE ROYAL NAVAL AIR SERVICE AND THE FLEET AIR ARM.
HE RODE UPON A CHERUB AND DID FLY: YEA HE DID FLY UPON THE WINGS OF THE WIND.

On both sides of the curved stone plinth are the names of 38 battles where the units fought.

# LONDON SW1

## The Guards Memorial

HORSE GUARDS PARADE, HORSE GUARDS ROAD SW1

GRADE I memorial unveiled in 1926 commemorates 14,000 Guardsmen who died in the First World War, and was added to after the Second World War. By architect Harold Chalton Bradshaw and sculptor Gilbert Ledward. The memorial stands 38ft 6". Portland stone with bronze relief panels and statuary.

Inscription reads TO THE GLORY OF GOD AND IN MEMORY OF THE OFFICERS WARRANT OFFICERS NON COMMISSIONED OFFICERS & GUARDSMEN OF HIS MAJESTY'S REGIMENTS OF FOOT GUARDS WHO GAVE THEIR LIVES FOR THEIR KING AND COUNTRY DURING THE GREAT WAR OF 1914 - 1918 AND OF THE OFFICERS WARRANT OFFICERS NON COMMISSIONED OFFICERS AND MEN OF THE HOUSEHOLD CAVALRY ROYAL REGIMENT OF ARTILLERY CORPS OF ROYAL ENGINEERS ROYAL ARMY SERVICE CORPS ROYAL ARMY MEDICAL CORPS AND OTHER UNITS WHO WHILE SERVING WITH THE GUARDS DIVISION IN FRANCE & BELGIUM 1915 - 1918 FELL WITH THEM IN THE FIGHT FOR THE WORLD'S FREEDOM.

Five bronze soldiers (7ft 3" high), one for each of the Guards regiments Grenadiers, Coldstreams, Scots, Welsh and Irish Guards represented, stand at ease against a stone cenotaph. Badges of the Guard's regiments are carved in relief below the figures with the following inscription THIS MEMORIAL ALSO COMMEMORATES ALL THOSE MEMBERS OF THE HOUSEHOLD DIVISION WHO DIED IN THE SECOND WORLD WAR AND IN THE SERVICE OF THEIR COUNTRY SINCE 1918. Bronze relief panels are mounted on either side of the cenotaph depicting various pieces of equipment specific to the regiments commemorated.

# LONDON SW1

## The Guards Crimean War Memorial
### WATERLOO PLACE SW1

GRADE II 1859-60 by John Bell. The Guards Crimean War Memorial commemorates the Allied victory in the Crimean War of 1853–56. Bronze statuary group cast from the cannons captured at the siege of Sevastopol on granite base and plinth. Rising above the group a symbolic figure of Honour on taller granite pedestal with 3 figures grouped in front representing Grenadier, Scots and Coldstream Guardsmen.

The statues of Sidney Herbert who was Secretary at War during the Crimean War and Florence Nightingale form subsidiary parts of the overall composition on island site in centre of road.

On either side of pedestal is a trophy of a highland targe with spike and battle honours - ALMA/ INKERMAN/ SEBASTAPOL written across. Inscription (north side) TO THE MEMORY OF 2162 OFFICERS, NON-COMD. OFFICERS AND PRIVATES OF THE BRIGADE OF GUARDS WHO FELL DURING THE WAR WITH RUSSIA 1854-5-6 ERECTED BY THEIR COMRADES (east and west sides) CRIMEA (plaque) THE GUARDS MEMORIAL WAS PULLED DOWN IN THE YEAR OF OUR LORD 1914 AND WAS RE-ERECTED 30 FEET NORTH OF ITS ORIGINAL POSITION IN ORDER TO PERMIT THE ERECTION OF THE FLORENCE NIGHTINGALE AND SIDNEY HERBERT STATUES.

# LONDON SW1

## Gurkha Memorial
HORSE GUARDS AVENUE SW1

The Memorial to the Brigade of Gurkhas was unveiled by Queen Elizabeth II on 3 December 1997. This was the first memorial to Gurkha soldiers in the United Kingdom, and was occasioned by transfer of their headquarters and training centre from Hong Kong to London in 1997. The sculptor was Philip Jackson, working from a statue of 1924 by Richard Reginald Goulden in the Foreign and Commonwealth Office, and the plinth was designed by Cecil Denny Highton.

Two casts of Goulden's sculpture had previously been erected in locations in Nepal as World War I memorials to the Gurkhas, the first at Kunraghat in 1928 and the second at Birpur in 1930. The memorial in London is more than one and a half times the size of this model, so Jackson worked the figure up in his own style and from a living model, Captain Khemkumar Limbu. One of several inscriptions on the plinth is a quotation from Sir Ralph Lilley Turner, a former officer in the 3rd Gurkha Rifles:

THE GURKHA SOLDIER
BRAVEST OF THE BRAVE MOST
GENEROUS OF THE GENEROUS
NEVER HAD COUNTRY MORE
FAITHFUL FRIENDS THANK YOU
Professor Sir Ralph Turner MC
(COMMEMORATES SERVICE OF
THE GURKHAS SINCE 1815
LISTING FORMATIONS AND
BATTALIONS AND CAMPAIGNS)

# LONDON SW1

## Iraq and Afghanistan Memorial

VICTORIA EMBANKMENT GARDENS SW1

The Iraq and Afghanistan Memorial commemorates British citizens who participated in the Gulf War, the Afghanistan War and the Iraq War in the period from 1990 to 2015. The Memorial gives equal prominence to military and civilian contributions, including the delivery of healthcare and humanitarian work. It is specifically intended to be inclusive of all those who contributed and therefore bears no names. Between 1990 and 2015, thousands of British citizens put themselves in harm's way, protected our nation's interests, helped those in danger and worked to improve the lives of those in other countries. 682 Service personnel lost their lives in the three conflicts. Civilians from a vast breadth of organisations worked for more than two decades in areas such as aid distribution, education, healthcare and governance to help the citizens of both Iraq and Afghanistan. The memorial designed by Paul Day and unveiled in 2017 consists of two large Portland stone monoliths. On one side, one stone is inscribed "AFGHANISTAN" and the other "IRAQ", and on the other side one bears the word "DUTY" and the other "SERVICE". One side of each stone is left in a rough condition as a reference to the rocky terrain of Afghanistan and Iraq. The stones are separated by a narrow gap and support between them a thick bronze medallion or tondo sculpted with reliefs that echo the memorial's theme of "duty and service", depicting members of the armed forces on one side and civilian workers on the other.

# LONDON SW1

## Korean War Memorial
VICTORIA EMBANKMENT GARDENS SW1

---

The Korean war memorial unveiled in 2014 was a gift from the Republic of Korea in honour of the 81,084 British Troops sent there. The carved obelisk of Portland stone on a base of Welsh slate stands 5.8 meters high, in front of which stands a bronze statue of a British soldier carved by Philip Jackson. The monument is engraved with a map and pictures of the landscape of the Korean Peninsula, as well as the national flags of Korea and Britain, and the British Korean Veterans Association's flag. Parts of the foundation of the memorial used stones from Pocheon in Gyeonggi-do Province where fierce battles occurred during the war.

Inscriptions on the pier THE KOREAN WAR - 1950-1953
In Korean and English:
WITH GRATITUDE FOR THE SACRIFICES MADE BY THE BRITISH ARMED FORCES IN DEFENCE OF FREEDOM AND DEMOCRACY IN THE REPUBLIC OF KOREA.
On the north face of the pier, below the UN symbol:
UNITED NATIONS
THE KOREAN WAR WAS THE FIRST UN ACTION AGAINST AGGRESSION. THE UN FORCES THAT FOUGHT THE NORTH KOREAN INVASION WERE DRAWN FROM 21 COUNTRIES. ALTHOUGH EXHAUSTED AND IMPOVERISHED AFTER THE SECOND WORLD WAR, BRITAIN RESPONDED IMMEDIATELY BY PROVIDING STRONG NAVAL, ARMY AND AIR FORCES AND BECAME THE SECOND LARGEST CONTRIBUTOR AFTER THE UNITED STATES. A DISTANT OBLIGATION HONOURABLY DISCHARGED.
On the back face of the pier: reliefs showing the Korean flag and the outline of the whole country.
On the south face of the pier, below the Union Jack:
BRITISH FORCES
IN THIS FIERCE AND BRUTAL CONFLICT THOSE WHO FOUGHT INCLUDED MANY SECOND WORLD WAR VETERANS REINFORCED BY RESERVISTS AND YOUNG NATIONAL SERVICEMEN. THE LAND BATTLE WAS FOUGHT AGAINST NUMERICALLY SUPERIOR COMMUNIST FORCES. THE TERRAIN WAS MOUNTAINOUS AND THE WEATHER EXTREME. 81,084 BRITISH SERVICEMEN SERVED IN THE THEATRE OF OPERATIONS. 1,106 WERE KILLED IN ACTION. THOUSANDS WERE WOUNDED AND 1,060 SUFFERED AS PRISONERS OF WAR.

# LONDON SW1

## The Rifle Brigade War Memorial

GROSVENOR GARDENS SW1

GRADE II* First World War regimental memorial. 1925 by John Tweed, with post-Second World War additions.
The Rifle Brigade was formed in 1800 as The Experimental Corps of Riflemen. In 1816 this body of men became The Rifle Brigade, winning various battle honours over the course of the C19. In 1966 The Rifle Brigade was merged with two other regiments to form The Royal Green Jackets. By 2007 The Royal Green Jackets had been reduced to two battalions and the regiment was merged with three others to form The Rifles. The Rifles is the largest infantry regiment in the modern British Army.
The memorial comprises a curving Portland stone screen wall with a central pylon which supports the life-sized bronze figure of a First World War rifleman marching forward helmeted and fully equipped. The terminal blocks are fronted by life-sized bronze figures: to the right an officer of 1800 and to the left a soldier of 1806. The figures are notable for their realism, and the contrast between the dynamic central figure and the relaxed stance of the flanking figures.
The regiment distinguished itself in both the Peninsular War and also the Waterloo Campaign.
On the central pylon the regimental badge is carved with the inscription IN MEMORY OF 11,575 OFFICERS WARRANT OFFICERS NON-COMMISSIONED OFFICERS AND RIFLEMEN OF THE RIFLE BRIGADE WHO FELL IN THE GREAT WAR 1914 - 1918.
A stone plaque was placed in front of the central pylon after the Second World War. The inscription reads AND IN MEMORY OF 1329 OFFICERS WARRANT OFFICERS NON-COMMISSIONED OFFICERS AND RIFLEMEN OF THE CORPS OF THE RIFLE BRIGADE WHO FELL IN THE WORLD WAR 1939-1945.

# LONDON SW1

## Royal Air Force Memorial
VICTORIA EMBANKMENT SW1

GRADE: II 1923 memorial dedicated to the memory of the casualties of the Royal Air Force in World War I (and, by extension, all subsequent conflicts).

The memorial comprises a Portland stone pylon topped by zodiacal globe bearing a gilded eagle, taken from the RAF's badge, with raised wings, facing towards France.

The pylon bears inscriptions on the sides facing the Embankment and to the river. Further inscriptions were added after the Second World War in 1946.

Around the top of the pylon, each face bears alternately the words PER ARDUA and AD ASTRA, from the motto of the RAF, "Per ardua ad astra" translates "Through Adversity to the Stars".

On the pylon facing the Embankment, there is the RAF insignia, and a dedication: IN MEMORY OF ALL RANKS OF THE ROYAL NAVAL AIR SERVICE ROYAL FLYING CORPS ROYAL AIR FORCE AND THOSE AIR FORCES FROM EVERY PART OF THE BRITISH EMPIRE WHO GAVE THEIR LIVES IN WINNING VICTORY FOR THEIR KING AND COUNTRY 1914–1918", and a quotation from Exodus, chapter 19: I BARE YOU ON EAGLES WINGS AND BROUGHT YOU UNTO MYSELF. Further down, on the base, is another inscription THIS INSCRIPTION IS ADDED IN REMEMBRANCE OF THOSE MEN AND WOMEN OF THE AIR FORCES OF EVERY PART OF THE BRITISH COMMONWEALTH AND EMPIRE WHO GAVE THEIR LIVES 1939–1945.

The side facing the river bears the RAF insignia again and the inscription: 1914/ 1918 IN PERPETUAL MEMORY 1939–1945.

# LONDON SW1

Royal Artillery Memorial                                      HYDE PARK CORNER SW1

GRADE I A prominently located memorial to one of the principal units of the British Army, which forms a testament to the role of artillery in the First World War. This is now internationally recognised as one of the finest memorials to have been erected anywhere after the First World War. Its combination of sculptural force, boldness of conception, vivid narrative and humanity makes the memorial pre-eminent.

The memorial commemorates the 49,076 fatalities suffered by the Royal Artillery (the single largest unit in the British Army) in the First World War, along with those in subsequent conflicts. Its stylised figures and reliefs convey the courage and endeavour required for front-line service in the Royal Artillery, while the howitzer is a vivid reminder of the role of fire power in the First World War.

Jagger was among the leading sculptors of his day, and won an enduring reputation for his war memorials. This monument's combination of heroism and humanity, and acknowledgment of the sacrifices demanded from wartime service, reflect Jagger's own experience as a decorated veteran of the war. The reliefs form the most powerful (and detailed) depictions of fighting on any war memorial in England, while the detailed representation of a huge gun was a daring rejection of traditional modes of commemoration.

The inclusion of an over-life size corpse was boldly direct and is also without parallel on any major British memorial.

The memorial is an outstanding example of a fully integrated architectural design with a strong sculptural element. The forms of the base form a fine support to the huge howitzer located above, and form a fine foil to the reliefs.

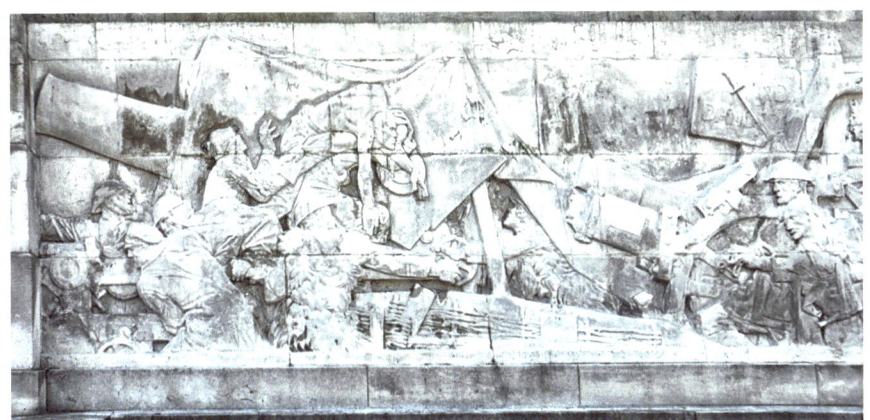

In 1919 The Royal Artillery War Commemoration Fund established a sub-committee for the erection of a war memorial. Early in 1921 it turned to the former infantry officer, Charles Sargeant Jagger MC, for a design which specifically depicted the role of artillery in the Great War. This was produced in association with the architect Lionel Pearson: a definitive design was presented in 1923. It was finally unveiled on 18 October 1925 by HRH Prince Arthur, Duke of Connaught. The memorial depicts a 9.2 inch howitzer, a form of heavy field gun introduced in 1914. Figures characteristic of the Royal Artillery stand on three sides. Artillery played a central role in combat in the First World War, with over 70% of casualties on the Western Front being caused by shellfire. Service in the Royal Artillery was extremely arduous too: the physical exertion required in operating guns is strongly sensed in the figural sculpture. Jagger combined detailed depictions of the actuality with combat with stylized relief sculptures. The recumbent corpse is a very rare feature on British war memorials. Having encountered initial reservations, Jagger was insistent on the inclusion of a dead Gunner and even offered to pay for the casting of this figure himself.

DESCRIPTION: Jagger's original conception consisted of "a very simple idea, a big powerful howitzer on a base which would be characteristic of an emplacement". Pearson designed a cruciform base on a several-stepped lower base. The four bronze figures depict (north) a recumbent corpse, draped in an overcoat; (south) an Artillery lieutenant, holding an overcoat; (east) a carrier, sporting shell panniers, with outstretched arms; and (west) a driver, wearing a cape and heavy protective boots. Around the principal level of the base is a frieze depicting front-line active service. North-east: a heavy battery of 60 pounder guns in action; south-east: anti-aircraft gunners; south-west: shell-spotting and signallers; north-west: bringing up a horse-drawn 13 pounder battery into action. On top of the base is a stone depiction of a 9.2 inch howitzer.

INSCRIPTIONS: east and west sides of the projecting arm of the base read, IN PROUD REMEMBRANCE OF THE FORTY NINE THOUSAND & SEVENTY SIX OF ALL RANKS OF THE ROYAL REGIMENT OF ARTILLERY WHO GAVE THEIR LIVES FOR KING AND COUNTRY IN THE GREAT WAR 1914-1919. Around the upper level of the base run the names of countries in which the RA served, FRANCE. AFRICA. PERSIA. EGYPT. CENTRAL ASIA. PALESTINE. RUSSIA. ITALY. INDIA. ARABIA. MESOPOTAMIA. FLANDERS. MACEDONIA. DARDANELLES.

Below the corpse is the inscription HERE WAS A ROYAL FELLOWSHIP OF DEATH, taken from Shakespeare's Henry V. On the north end is a further inscription referring to the roll of honour buried below. To the south are additional inscription panels commemorating the 29,924 losses of the regiment in the Second World War, added in 1949.

## Royal Artillery Boer War Memorial　　THE MALL SW1

GRADE: II* A regimental war memorial of 1906-10. Designed by Aston Webb and William Colton. Portland stone memorial, with bronze sculpture and relief panels. To the rear of the monument is a wall with a series of bronze plaques forming a frieze with the following wording in relief: 'ERECTED BY THE OFFICERS AND MEN OF THE ROYAL ARTILLERY IN MEMORY OF THEIR HONOURED DEAD. SOUTH AFRICA. 1899-1902'. Terminating the wall at either side are stone piers which bear bronze plaques showing scenes of war in high relief; soldiers of the regiment transporting their arms over hilly terrain, and the Royal Artillery Corps in action. To their flanks are further bronze plaques with the names of the fallen in relief. At the centre of the raised plinth is a square pedestal with chamfered corners. This has a deeply moulded entablature, the frieze of which represents gun carriages and horses at the gallop in high relief. Above the projecting plinth is a further band of bronze relief which shows the regimental mottos: 'UBIQUE' (Everywhere) and 'QUO. FAS ET GLORIA DUCUNT ' (Where Right and Glory lead). To the top of the pedestal is a sculpted bronze group, showing the winged figure of Peace controlling a horse (representative of War) by its bridle.

# LONDON SW1

## Royal Marines National Memorial
### THE MALL SW1

GRADE: II Erected in memory of Royal Marines who died in the Boxer Rebellion Campaign in China and the Boer War in southern Africa. 1903 by Sir T. Jackson and Adrian Jones. Two bronze figures on carved Portland stone base with bronze plaques and reliefs, commemorating Royal Marines killed in South Africa and China. Wounded marine with comrade standing over him defending him with levelled rifle and bayonet. Surmounts pedestal which has bronze plaques: Corps badge, relief depictions of action at Graspan and repulse of Chinese attack on Peking.
Carved dolphins on each corner symbolise naval service.
Inscription front face: ERECTED BY THE OFFICERS AND MEN OF THE ROYAL MARINES IN MEMORY OF THEIR COMRADES WHO WERE KILLED IN ACTION OR DIED OF WOUNDS OR DISEASE IN SOUTH AFRICA AND CHINA 1899 - 1900
Back face: SOUTH AFRICA CHINA (NAMES)
Bronze ring on ground around memorial: THIS MEMORIAL WAS REDEDICATED IN OCTOBER 2000 IN HONOUR OF ALL ROYAL MARINES WHO HAVE SERVED THEIR COUNTRY BY LAND AND SEA AND WHO ARE FOREVER REMEMBERED BY THEIR FRIENDS

# LONDON SW1

## The Royal Naval Division War Memorial
HORSE GUARDS PARADE SW1

GRADE: II* 1925 memorial by Sir Edwin Landseer Lutyens, carvings by Eric R Broadbent and Frederick J Wilcoxson. The Memorial is dedicated to the 45,000 members of the Royal Naval Division who died during World War I.

The obelisk is carved in relief with the insignia of the Division, whilst below, water spouts from the mouths of carved lions heads. The square plinth is decorated with small square incised panels, each bearing the badge of units which served in the Division, nine on each side.

Panels bear the inscriptions: Salonica 1916,/ France and Belgium 1916-1918,/ In memory of the officers and other ranks of the Royal Naval Division 1914 and 1918,/ Antwerp 1914,/ Gallipoli 1915-16. The central panel contains a verse by Rupert Brooke BLOW OUT YOU BUGLES OVER THE RICH DEAD THERE'S NONE OF THESE SO LONELY AND POOR OF OLD BUT, DYING, HAS MADE US RARER GIFTS THAN GOLD THESE LAID THE WORLD AWAY, POURED OUT THE RED SWEET WINE OF YOUTH, GAVE UP THE YEARS TO BE OF WORK AND JOY, AND THAT UNHOPED SERENE, THAT MEN CALL AGE. AND THOSE WHO WOULD HAVE BEEN THEIR SONS THEY GAVE THEIR IMMORTALITY. RUPERT BROOKE 1887-1915 / HOOD BATTALION.

On the extension of the memorial is the following inscription THIS MEMORIAL DESIGNED BY SIR EDWIN LUTYENS WAS UNVEILED ON THE HORSE GUARDS PARADE AT THE CORNER OF THE ADMIRALTY ON APRIL 25TH 1925 THE TENTH ANNIVERSARY OF THE LANDING ON GALLIPOLI . Below this is inscribed REMOVED IN 1940, ERECTED IN GREENWICH IN 1951 AND REINSTATED ON THIS SITE IN 2003.

## Royal Tank Regiment Memorial

WHITEHALL COURT SW1

The statue depicts the crew of a World War 2 Comet tank which was issued to the Royal Tank Regiment in 1945. The memorial shows the unique comradeship which exists among the men who fight in tanks. Sculpted by Vivien Mallock, ARBS from the original design by the late G. H. Paulin, ARSA RIBS RI. Unveiled in 2000.

9 foot bronze. A tall bronze sculpture of five members of a WW2 comet tank crew, standing in line but looking off to their left. They wear battle dress and berets, and each holds an item of equipment: besa machine gun, gun sight, field glasses etc. The sculpture is stood on a circular stone plinth surrounded by deep circular platform.

Inscription on base of figures FROM MUD, THROUGH BLOOD, TO THE GREEN FIELDS BEYOND

Below plinth: In tribute to the Crewmen who have served in the Heavy Section and Heavy Branch Machine Gun Corps the Tank Corps Royal Tank Corps and Royal Tank Regiment since tanks were first used in combat at Flers on 15th September 1916. On panel set into the paved surround: ROYAL TANK REGIMENT MEMORIAL STATUE THIS MEMORIAL STATUE DEPICTS THE CREW OF A WORLD WAR 2 COMET TANK WHICH WAS ISSUED TO THE ROYAL TANK REGIMENT IN 1945 THE COMET HAD A CREW OF FIVE; COMMANDER, GUNNER, LOADER, HULL MACHINE GUNNER, DRIVER. IT WAS EQUIPPED WITH A 77MM HIGH VELOCITY GUN AND POWERED BY A 600 HORSE POWER ROLLS ROYCE ENGINE. THE COMET PROVED TO BE HIGHLY EFFECTIVE AGAINST ENEMY TANKS OF THE DAY    FEAR NAUGHT

# LONDON SW1

## The Unknown Warrior
WESTMINSTER ABBEY SW1

At the west end of the Nave of Westminster Abbey is the grave of the Unknown Warrior, whose body was brought from France to be buried here on 11 November 1920. The grave, which contains soil from France, is covered by a slab of black Belgian marble from a quarry near Namur. On it is the following inscription, engraved with brass from melted down wartime ammunition:

BENEATH THIS STONE RESTS THE BODY OF A BRITISH WARRIOR UNKNOWN BY NAME OR RANK BROUGHT FROM FRANCE TO LIE AMONG THE MOST ILLUSTRIOUS OF THE LAND AND BURIED HERE ON ARMISTICE DAY 11 NOV: 1920, IN THE PRESENCE OF HIS MAJESTY KING GEORGE V HIS MINISTERS OF STATE THE CHIEFS OF HIS FORCES AND A VAST CONCOURSE OF THE NATION THUS ARE COMMEMORATED THE MANY MULTITUDES WHO DURING THE GREAT WAR OF 1914-1918 GAVE THE MOST THAT MAN CAN GIVE LIFE ITSELF FOR GOD FOR KING AND COUNTRY FOR LOVED ONES HOME AND EMPIRE FOR THE SACRED CAUSE OF JUSTICE AND THE FREEDOM OF THE WORLD THEY BURIED HIM AMONG THE KINGS BECAUSE HE HAD DONE GOOD TOWARD GOD AND TOWARD HIS HOUSE

Around the main inscription are four texts:
(top) THE LORD KNOWETH THEM THAT ARE HIS,
(sides) GREATER LOVE HATH NO MAN THAN THIS UNKNOWN AND YET WELL KNOWN, DYING AND BEHOLD WE LIVE,
(base) IN CHRIST SHALL ALL BE MADE ALIVE.

The idea of a Tomb of the Unknown Warrior was first conceived in 1916 by the Reverend David Railton, who, while serving as an army chaplain on the Western Front, had seen a grave marked by a rough cross, which bore the pencil-written legend 'An Unknown British Soldier'.

He wrote to the Dean of Westminster in 1920 proposing that an unidentified British soldier from the battlefields in France be buried with due ceremony in Westminster Abbey "amongst the kings" to represent the many hundreds of thousands of Empire dead.

The body was chosen from unknown British servicemen exhumed from four battle areas, the Aisne, the Somme, Arras and Ypres.

The body of the Unknown Warrior may be from any of the three services, Army, Navy or Air Force, and from any part of the British Isles, Dominions or Colonies and represents all those who died who have no other memorial or known grave.

# LONDON SW1

## The Women of World War II

WHITEHALL SW1

Bronze cenotaph, by John W. Mills, around which hang seventeen uniforms representing the different services performed by 7 million women during WW2, including Land Army, canteen ladies overalls, Wren uniform, nursing cape, welders helmet, a police overcoat. The monument stands 22 feet(6.7m) high, 16 feet (4.9m) long and 6 feet(1.8m) wide. The lettering on the sides replicates the typeface used on war time ration books. Inscriptions: THE WOMEN OF WORLD WAR II; This memorial was raised to commemorate the vital work done by nearly seven million women in World War II; Unveiled by Her Majesty the Queen July 9 2005, on the 60th anniversary of the end of World War II.

# LONDON SW2

## African and Caribbean War Memorial
WINDRUSH SQUARE SW2

The memorial was unveiled in Windrush Square on 22 June 2017 – Windrush Day. The date of the arrival of SS Empire Windrush in 1948 carrying 498 men and a few women from the Caribbean. They had responded to the call to help rebuild Britain after the devastations of World War Two. The Windrush Generation made a huge contribution to rebuilding the country following the war.

This memorial comprising of two obelisks carries the names of every regiment, force, contingent and troop from Africa and the Caribbean. Inscription - IN MEMORY OF THE SERVICE MEN AND WOMEN FROM AFRICA AND THE CARIBBEAN WHO SERVED ALONGSIDE THE FORCES OF THE BRITISH COMMONWEALTH AND HER ALLIES DURING WW1 AND WW2. REMEMBERING THE FORGOTTEN.

The African and Caribbean War Memorial is the first of its kind in the United Kingdom, to specifically honour Commonwealth soldiers from Africa and the Caribbean. Black Britons volunteered at recruitment centres to serve in the Army and Navy soon after Britain joined WW1. They were joined by volunteers from the Caribbean, many of whom paid for their own passage. The West Indies not only contributed men to the war effort but people from the islands made significant donations despite economic hardship. It is estimated that 10,000 Africans were killed with 166 receiving awards for bravery. More than 2 million African and Caribbean Military Servicemen and Servicewomen participated in WWI and WWII. Some 16,000 men and women from the Caribbean volunteered for the British Armed Forces. Around 6,000 served with the Royal Air Force and the Royal Canadian Air Force working as fighter pilots, technicians, air gunners and ground staff.

# LONDON SW3

## 6th Dragoon Guards (The Carabiniers)     CHELSEA EMBANKMENT SW3

Commissioned by the Regiment through public subscription and dedicated in 1905.

Three sided red brick and bath stone screen with bronze panels, metal railings to the front and sides. Bronze relief plaque depicts mounted trooper holding three horses whilst his three comrades skirmish on a kopse in the near distance.
Inscription: SOUTH AFRICAN WAR THE CARABINIERS 1899 - 1902.
IN MEMORY OF THE OFFICERS, N. C. OFFICERS AND MEN OF THE VI. DRAGOON GUARDS, (THE CARABINIERS) WHO GAVE THEIR LIVES FOR THEIR COUNTRY IN THE SOUTH AFRICAN WAR. 1899 - 1902. ERECTED BY PAST AND PRESENT CARABINIERES. AD 1905

Plaque side : RELIEF OF KIMBERLEY PAARDEBURG. DRIEFONTEIN. JOHANNESBURG. DIAMOND HILL. BELFAST &C OFFICERS, N. C. OFFICERS AND MEN KILLED IN ACTION (NAMES)
Plaque: DIED OF WOUNDS OR DISEASE. (NAMES)
The Carabiniers (6th Dragoon Guards) was a cavalry regiment of the British Army. It was formed in 1685 as the Lord Lumley's Regiment of Horse. It was renamed as His Majesty's 1st Regiment of Carabiniers in 1740, the 3rd Regiment of Horse (Carabiniers) in 1756 and the 6th Regiment of Dragoon Guards in 1788. After two centuries of service, including the First World War, the regiment was amalgamated with the 3rd Dragoon Guards (Prince of Wales's) to form the 3rd/6th Dragoon Guards in 1922.

# LONDON SW6

### Fulham War Memorial
VICARAGE GARDENS,
PUTNEY BRIDGE APPROACH SW6

---

Grade: II   1921 by Alfred Turner. Bronze figure of Peace on a Portland stone pedestal and three-stepped base. On the front of the pedestal is the figure of a cherub knelling in front of a cross.
The inscriptions are carved into the front of the pedestal and read: 'TO THE HONOUR OF FULHAM'S GALLANT DEAD',
'THEY DIED FOR FREEDOM', '1914-1918' and '1939-1945'. The memorial was originally erected in 1920 on Fulham Palace Road. In 1934 it was moved to Vicarage Gardens.

### Fulham (All Saints) War Memorial
ALL SAINTS CHURCHYARD
PUTNEY BRIDGE APPROACH SW6

---

Grade: II   War memorial in the form of a canopied cross commemorates parishioners who died during the Great War. Unveiled in 1923. It was designed to mirror the main doorway to the church. There are no names on the memorial as these are recorded separately inside the church,.
Oak cross with bronze sculpture of Christ and INRI scroll. This rests on a platform of Portland stone, the front face of which has the bronze inscription "1914 - 1918". Over the cross is an elaborate Portland stone crocketed canopy, with crown design to the front, supported by four pinnacled columns.

# LONDON SW7

## Twelve Responses to Tragedy/ Yalta Memorial CROMWELL GARDENS SW7

Twelve Responses to Tragedy, or the Yalta Memorial, remembers those people who were forcibly repatriated by the Allies to Eastern Europe and the Soviet Union after the Second World War as a result of the Yalta Conference at the conclusion of the Second World War. Many did not survive the journey home and those that did faced starvation and disease. Created by the British sculptor Angela Conner. The memorial was dedicated in 1986.

The memorial consists of a stone column upon a brick plinth, upon the column sits a bronze bust of 12 conjoined heads of men, women, and children.

Inscription on stone reads: THIS SCULPTURE WAS DEDICATED BY THE BISHOP OF FULHAM ON 2ND AUGUST 1986 TO REPLACE THE PREVIOUS MEMORIAL DEDICATED BY THE BISHOP OF LONDON ON 6TH MARCH 1982 WHICH WAS LATER DESTROYED BY VANDALS TO WHOM THE TRUTH WAS INTOLERABLE

An inscription on a curved stone plinth reads: THIS MEMORIAL WAS PLACED HERE BY MEMBERS OF ALL PARTIES IN BOTH HOUSES OF THE PARLIAMENT AND BY MANY OTHER SYMPATHISERS IN MEMORY OF THE COUNTLESS INNOCENT MEN WOMEN AND CHILDREN FROM THE SOVIET UNION AND OTHER EAST EUROPEAN STATES WHO WERE IMPRISONED AND DIED AT THE HANDS OF COMMUNIST GOVERNMENTS AFTER BEING REPATRIATED AT THE CONCLUSION OF THE SECOND WORLD WAR MAY THEY REST IN PEACE

The inscription on the memorial was personally approved by Margaret Thatcher during her tenure as Prime Minister. The memorial has been described as a war memorial as it was created in response to events that arose out of the conclusion of the Second World War.

# LONDON SW11

## 24th East Surrey Division
BATTERSEA PARK SW11

GRADE II* WWI memorial. Designed and sculpted by Eric Henri Kennington RA. Portland stone. Consists of the figures of three infantry soldiers with helmets rifles and full kit, with a serpent at their feet, standing upon a three part columnar base.

The figure to the left was modelled on the poet and writer Robert Graves, author of the outstanding war memoir 'Goodbye to All That'.

The base of the memorial has the inscription, XXIV Division France 1914-1918 around the top, with the twenty unit badges beneath.

The memorial commemorates over 10,000 men who had been killed or listed as `missing presumed dead' whilst serving with the 24th Infantry Division. The memorial was unveiled on 4 October 1924 in an opening ceremony performed by Field Marshall Plumer and the Bishop of Southwark.

# LONDON W1

## The 7 July Memorial　　　　　　　　　　　　　　　　HYDE PARK W1

A permanent memorial to honour the victims of the 7 July 2005 London Bombings. The memorial comprises 52 stainless steel pillars (stelae), representing each of the 52 victims, grouped together in four inter-linking clusters reflecting the four locations of the incidents. An inscription carried at eye-level describing the date, exact timing and location of each life lost is placed on each of the stelae. A stainless steel plaque listing the names of the victims is sited on a grass bank at the far eastern end of the memorial.

Working closely with the families of the victims of the 7 July 2005 bombings, a permanent memorial was designed to commemorate the worst terrorist attacks in peacetime London.

The 7 July Memorial was unveiled in Hyde Park by Their Royal Highnesses, The Prince of Wales and The Duchess of Cornwall, in a ceremony attended by senior political figures and the families of the 52 killed, on the fourth anniversary of the disaster, Tuesday 7 July 2009.

# LONDON W1

## Animals in War Memorial

BROOK GATE W1

This monument by David Backhouse is a tribute to all the animals that served, suffered and died alongside the British, Commonwealth and Allied forces in the wars and conflicts of the 20th century. It was unveiled in November 2004, the 90th anniversary of the start of World War I.
Constructed in Portland stone and cast bronze, 58ft (17.68m) wide and 55ft (16.76m) deep.
There are three principal elements in the design; two different levels and a dominating and powerful wall between them. On the lower level, two heavily laden bronze mules struggle through an arena, enclosed by the dominant wall symbolising the war experience. The mules approach a flight of steps that leads through the wall. Beyond the wall, on the upper level, a bronze horse and dog stand facing north into the gardens.
The Wall: Images of the many different animals used in 20th century conflicts are depicted in bas-relief on the inside of the longer section of wall. On the outside of this wall a line of ghostly silhouettes is carved, representing the animals lost in the conflicts. Beneath the main heading "Animals in War", the memorial has two inscriptions: "THIS MONUMENT IS DEDICATED TO ALL THE ANIMALS THAT SERVED AND DIED ALONGSIDE BRITISH AND ALLIED FORCES IN WARS AND CAMPAIGNS THROUGHOUT TIME." The second reads: "THAY HAD NO CHOICE."
The British, Commonwealth and Allied forces enlisted many millions of animals to serve and often die alongside their armies. These animals were chosen for a variety of their natural instincts and vast numbers were killed, often suffering agonising deaths from wounds, starvation, thirst, exhaustion, disease and exposure.
Eight million horses and countless mules and donkeys died in the First World War. They were used to transport ammunition and supplies to the front and many died, not only from shellfire but also in terrible weather and appalling conditions. Mules were found to have tremendous stamina in extreme climates and over the most difficult terrain, serving courageously in the freezing mud on the Western Front and later at Monte Cassino in World War II. Equally they toiled unflinchingly in the oppressive heat of Burma, Eritrea and Tunisia.
The dog's innate qualities of intelligence and devotion were valued and used by the forces in conflicts throughout the century. They ran messages, laid telegraph wires, detected mines, dug out bomb victims and acted as guard or patrol

dogs. Many battled on despite horrific wounds and in terrifying circumstances to the limit of their endurance. More than 100,000 pigeons served Britain in the First World War and 200,000 in World War II. They saved thousands of lives by carrying vital messages, over long distances, when other methods of communication were impossible. Flying at the rate of a mile a minute from the front line, from behind enemy lines or from ships or planes, they would struggle on through all weathers, even when severely wounded and exhausted, in order to carry their vital messages home. Other animals: Elephants, camels, oxen, bullocks, cats, canaries, even glow worms - all contributed their strength, energy and their lives in times of war and conflict.

# LONDON W1

## Cavalry of the Empire Memorial

HYDE PARK W1

GRADE: II* The Cavalry Memorial unveiled in May 1924, designed by Adrian Jones, an army vet, the sculpture contains bronze which came from guns captured during World War One. The base was designed by Sir John Burnet.

During the First World War the cavalry's traditional role was undermined by the development of the aeroplane for scouting and reconnaissance, and by new weaponry such as the machine gun, poisoned gas and, from 1916, armoured tanks. Even so, during the First World war the cavalry arm of the British Expeditionary Force, which often served as foot soldiers in the trenches, suffered 19,051 casualties of whom 4,421 were fatalities; the ratio of officer deaths was greater than in the Infantry.

The design is based on the patron saint of the cavalry (as well as of England), St George, together with a dragon, and includes a bronze tablet listing the 150 Cavalry units which took part in the war. The text has been updated to include later conflicts.

The statue stands on a rectangular base, whose upper part is also in bronze and carries a frieze depicting imperial cavalry, Indian and South African as well as British.

The lower part of the base carries the inscription ERECTED BY THE CAVALRY OF THE EMPIRE IN MEMORY OF COMRADES WHO GAVE THEIR LIVES IN THE WAR 1914 1919 ALSO IN THE WAR 1939-1945 AND ON ACTIVE SERVICE THEREAFTER

# LONDON W1

## Eagle Squadrons Memorial
GROSVENOR SQUARE GARDENS W1

GRADE: II  The Eagle Squadron Memorial, 1985 by Dame Elisabeth Frink commemorates the sacrifices made by American citizens who were willing to renounce their citizenship to fight in the Second World War. In the United States it was illegal for citizens to join the armed forces of foreign nations; the penalty was loss of citizenship, but despite this, large numbers volunteered and flew with the RAF prior to the participation of the US in the war.

The memorial was commissioned for Grosvenor Square, home to the US Embassy and a number of other memorials to American historic figures and events.

The memorial consists of an obelisk with a tapering top surmounted by an eagle in flight. The figurative eagle is roughly moulded with a deeply textured surface finish; the feet appear oversized, and the head is painted white, rendering it recognisable as the American bald eagle.

The square shaft is inscribed with incised lettering on each side.

On the north-facing front is the stylised emblem of a spread eagle as seen on the Great Seal of the United States, clutching arrows in its left claw and an olive branch in its right, with the inscription 'EAGLE SQUADRONS
THIS MEMORIAL IS TO THE MEMORY OF THE 244 AMERICAN AND 16 BRITISH FIGHTER PILOTS AND OTHER PERSONNEL WHO SERVED IN THE THREE ROYAL AIR FORCE EAGLE SQUADRONS PRIOR TO THE PARTICIPATION OF THE UNITED STATES OF AMERICA IN THE SECOND WORLD WAR
THEY SERVED WITH VALOR
FOUNDED BY CHARLES F SWEENY, JUNE 1940
ERECTED THROUGH THE GENEROSITY OF THE HEARST CORPORATION OF AMERICA IN THE NAME OF WILLIAM RANDOLPH HEARST PUBLISHER'.

The other faces commemorate each of the three squadrons: Squadron 133 on the east, with an emblem of a spread eagle on a bed of stars, and the motto, 'LET US TO THE BATTLE'; Squadron 121 on the south with a carved crest showing a Native American at the centre, and the motto, 'FOR LIBERTY', and on the west, Squadron 71 has a carved spread eagle crest and the motto 'FIRST FROM THE EYRIES'.

The names, rank and decoration of the 289 subjects, of whom 71 died, are ordered by regiment and surname.

# Machine Gun Corps Memorial
HYDE PARK CORNER W1

GRADE: II* 1925. Francis Derwent Wood, sculptor. This memorial commemorates the 15,552 fatalities suffered by the Machine Gun Corps from its raising in 1915 until its disbanding in 1922. Its front-line exposure to danger won it the nickname of 'The Suicide Club'.

The memorial comprises a standing naked figure holding a two-handed sword, representing David. He stands on a tall pedestal of pale grey Italian marble, to which are attached lower wings: on these stand two real Vickers machine guns, encased in bronze and laurel-wreathed around the gun barrel. Beneath each is a tin helmet, and a tool bag.

The front of the central pedestal is inscribed "ERECTED TO COMMEMORATE THE GLORIOUS HEROES OF THE MACHINE GUN CORPS WHO FELL IN THE GREAT WAR" "Saul hath slain his thousands but David his tens of thousands". MCMXIV - MCMXIX {1914 - 1919}

On the rear of plinth:
The Machine Gun Corps of which His Majesty King George V was Colonel-in-Chief, was formed by royal warrant dated the 14th day of October 1915. The corps served in France, Flanders, Russia, Italy, Egypt, Palestine, Mesopotamia, Salonica, India, Afghanistan and East Africa. The last unit of the Corps to be disbanded was the depot at Shorncliffe on the 15th day of July 1922. The total number who served in the Corps was some 11,500 officers, and 159,000 other ranks of whom 1,120 officers and 12,671 other ranks were killed and 2,881 officers and 45,377 other ranks were wounded, missing or prisoners of war.

# LONDON W1

## Marylebone War Memorial
BRYANSTONE STREET W1

GRADE: II Dedicated around 1920 to the sacrifice made by the members of the local community who lost their lives in the First World War. It commemorates 69 local servicemen who died. The memorial is in the form of a teak Calvary cross set within its original corner enclosure. The figure of Christ is gilded. Designer: Sir Walter Tapper. Inscription - OF YOUR CHARITY PRAY FOR THESE WHO GAVE THEIR LIVES IN THE GREAT WAR 1914 – 1918 R.I.P THEIR NAME LIVETH FOR EVERMORE. Behind the cross are two arch-headed Portland stone plaques on the wall of the church bearing the names of the fallen.

# LONDON W1

## New Zealand War Memorial

HYDE PARK CORNER W1

The New Zealand Memorial called The Southern Stand dedicated on 11 November 2006 commemorates the enduring bonds between New Zealand and the United Kingdom, and the shared sacrifice during times of war. It is a symbol both of our common heritage and of New Zealand's distinct identity. Thousands of soldiers from New Zealand served with the British Army during the First and Second World Wars.

Designed by architect John Hardwick-Smith and sculptor Paul Dibble the memorial consists of 16 cross-shaped vertical bronze 'standards' set out in formation on a grassy slope. The memorial is positioned where the main pedestrian route runs through the memorial so that visitors will walk amongst the sculptures, encouraging people to stop and explore. The dark patinated surfaces of the standards are adorned with different texts, patterns and small sculptures, all symbolic of New Zealand, including fern shapes, a manaia figure, plants and animals from New Zealand, emblems of the New Zealand armed forces, and references to authors and artists from New Zealand.

The standards have different heights, with the ends cut off at a diagonal so they resemble cross-like grave markers from a distance.

Nine of the standards form in a regular grid pattern, with a tenth as a leader. The formal arrangement is intended to resemble a group of soldiers in procession, Pouwhenua markers around Māori ancestral sites, or Celtic standing stones.

Six standards are positioned beyond the main group and are arranged to form the shape of the Southern Cross constellation. At night, their tops are illuminated so that the crosses appear like the southern stars, indicating the compass direction south … and pointing the way home for wandering Kiwis. From afar, they appear like a series of crosses hanging in the air, with some of the atmosphere of the soldiers' mass cemeteries.

The forward-leaning angle of the standards gives them a defiant pose "reminiscent of warriors during haka, the defensive bat in cricket, and the barrel of a shouldered gun".

# LONDON W1

## RAF Bomber Command Memorial

GREEN PARK along PICCADILLY W1

Iconic stone monument honoring 55,573 aircrew who died flying Bomber Command during World War II. Designed by Liam O'Connor.

The monument has as its centre a sculpture by Philip Jackson in bronze of seven men, a typical bomber crew: Pilot, Navigator, Flight Engineer, Mid-Upper Gunner, Bomb Aimer, Rear Gunner, Wireless Operator; young but weary after tense hours over enemy territory, parachute packs in hand. Five scan the sky for friends who may or may not return; two look to the ground, reflecting on another night survived. Within the memorial, the space is open to the sky with an opening designed to allow light to fall directly onto sculptures of the aircrew. The design for the roof incorporates sections of aluminium recovered from a Handley Page Halifax III bomber shot down over Belgium on the night of 12 May 1944, in which eight crew were killed. Three members of the crew were still at their stations when the aircraft was excavated in 1997. They were buried in Belgium with full military honours alongside the five other members of the crew. The memorial was officially unveiled by Her Majesty The Queen on 28 June 2012.

RAF Bomber Command was formed in 1936. More than 125,00 men flew in Bomber Command and all were volunteers. Of this number nearly half lost their lives. Most who flew were very young, the great majority still in their late teens. Crews came from across the globe – from the UK, Canada, Australia, New Zealand and all corners of the Commonwealth, as well as from occupied nations including Poland, France and Czechoslovakia.

Flying at night over occupied Europe, running the gauntlet of German night fighters, anti-aircraft fire and mid-air collisions, the nerves of these young men were stretched to breaking point.

The famous 'Dam Busters' raid of May 1943 shocked the world with its audacity, as Guy Gibson's 617 Squadron launched a daring raid on the dams surrounding the Ruhr Valley.

Other attacks, like that on the battleship Tirpitz the following year, eliminated the German navy's last major surface ship. Raids in 1944 and 1945 against German 'V weapon' launch sites were also a crucial defensive measure, helping to limit attacks from flying bombs and rockets on British cities.

All these operations demonstrated the adaptability of Bomber Command crews, taking on precision strikes with great effect.

Over 1000 aircraft and 7000 aircrew were lost during the 'Battle of Berlin'.

In early 1944 Bomber Command helped to pave the way for D-Day, the allied invasion of occupied Europe. Bomber Command aircraft played a vital and highly effective role attacking infrastructure around the invasion beaches. Attacking railways, roads and other transport links created chaos behind German lines, preventing the defending forces from massing to repel the landings. The closing months of the war saw operations, such as the raid on Dresden in February 1945. In four huge raids by the RAF and United States Army Air Force, a firestorm destroyed the city centre and killed thousands of civilians. 1945 also saw another, lesser known mission. From 29 April to 7 May Operation Manna saw Bomber Command crews drop food supplies to the starving people of occupied Holland. Flying at 500 feet in broad daylight over hostile territory, the crews brought vital relief to the civilian population.

# LONDON W2

## Great Western Railway War Memorial
ON PLATFORM 1, PADDINGTON RAILWAY STATION, PRAED STREET W2

Memorial to the memory of employees of the Great Western Railway who died during the First World War. The stonework was designed by the architect Thomas S. Tait, and the bronze figure by the sculptor Charles Sargeant Jagger; the memorial was unveiled on Armistice Day in 1922.

Its dominant feature is a large bronze statue of a British First World War soldier dressed in battle gear, wearing a helmet, woollen scarf, and a greatcoat draped over his shoulders. The soldier is looking down, reading a letter from home.

On the stone surround are two stylised reliefs of the emblems of the Royal Navy and the Royal Air Force. Inside the plinth was placed a sealed casket, containing a vellum roll upon which were inscribed the names of the men who gave their lives.

Inscription: IN HONOUR OF THOSE WHO SERVED IN THE WORLD WARS 1914 † 1918   1939 † 1945 3312 MEN AND WOMEN OF THE GREAT WESTERN RAILWAY GAVE THEIR LIVES FOR KING AND COUNTRY.

Inside the waiting room behind the memorial is a plaque marking the unveiling of the memorial. Inscription: THE GREAT WESTERN RAILWAY WAR MEMORIAL ON PLATFORM No 1 IMMEDIATELY OUTSIDE THIS ROOM WAS UNVEILED ON ARMISTICE DAY, SATURDAY, NOVEMBER 11TH 1922 BY THE RT. HON VISCOUNT CHURCHILL, G.C.V.O. AND DEDICATED BY HIS GRACE THE ARCHBISHOP OF CANTERBURY. THE BRONZE FIGURE WAS EXECUTED BY MR CS. JAGGER M.C. R.B.S AND THE ARCHITECTURAL WORK BY MR TS. TAIT A.R.I.B.A.

# LONDON W2

## Lancaster Gate Memorial Cross
LANCASTER GATE W2

GRADE II  A City of Westminster information plaque on the ground at the centre of the traffic island provides the following:
The Christ Church war memorial commemorates those residents of the Metropolitan Borough of Paddington who sacrificed their lives during the Great War (1914 -1918). Designed by Sir Walter Tapper RA and sculpted by Lawrence A Turner, the memorial was erected on the footpath outside Christ Church and originally unveiled on 27 March 1921 by the Bishop of Kensington. The memorial is in the gothic style.
The tabernacle below the gilded metal crucifix accommodates eight niches with statues. The figures are of St. George of England, St. Louis of France & the warrior saints of Christendom, being Maurice; Longinus; Victor; Adrian, Florian and Eustace. The grade II listed memorial was severely damaged during the storms of October 1987. Westminster City Council has restored the monument and moved it to its present location as part of the Lancaster Gate street improvement scheme. The restored memorial was unveiled on 11 November 2002.

## Katyn Massacre

GUNNERSBURY CEMETERY, GUNNERSBURY PARK W3 8LE

Unveiled on 18 September 1976, this Katyn memorial was the first in the world. It was erected in the face of opposition from both the Soviet and English governments. Designed by Louis Fitzgibbon and Count Stefan Zamoyski. Granite obelisk, with two crossed wreaths Eagle encircled with barbed wire.

Inscription KATYN 1940 (Polish inscription: 'THE CONSCIENCE OF THE WORLD CALLS FOR A VERIFICATION OF THE TRUTH')
IN REMEMBRANCE OF 14,500 POLISH PRISONERS OF WAR WHO DISAPPEARED IN 1940 FROM CAMPS AT KOZIELSK, STAROBIELSK AND OSTASZKOW OF WHOM 4,500 WERE LATER IDENTIFIED IN A MASS GRAVE AT KATYN NEAR SMOLENSK.

The wording on the plaques is: THIS CASKET CONTAINS SOIL FROM THEIR GRAVES MURDERED BY THE SOVIET SECRET POLICE ON STALIN'S ORDERS 1940. THE SOIL HEREUNDER CAME FROM THEIR GRAVEYARD 1990
AS FINALLY ADMITTED IN APRIL 1990, BY THE U.S.S.R. AFTER 50 YEARS SHAMEFUL DENIAL OF THE TRUTH.

The Soviet Union captured 180,000 Polish soldiers during its invasion of Poland in 1939. Most were herded off to slave-camps in Siberia, but 22,000 officers were not. In April 1940, on Stalin's orders, each was executed with a single shot to the back of the head. The victims included approximately 8000 Polish army officers taken prisoner during the Soviet invasion of Poland in 1939, another 6000 were police officers and the rest were Polish intelligentsia, university lecturers, doctors, lawyers, officials, priests and others considered to be members of the "bourgeoisie".

The bulk of the victims were interned at three Soviet camps (Kozielsk, Starobielsk and Ostaszków) before being taken to NKVD mass murder sites, where they were killed and buried in mass graves. The graves of the Kozielsk prisoners were found in 1943 in mass graves at Katyn forest near Smolensk in the Soviet Union. The fate of the other victims and the location of their graves was not known until five decades later.

However, neither the Soviet government nor successive governments of Russia have ever permitted a full investigation of the massacre, and none of the perpetrators of this war crime have ever been brought to justice.

# LONDON W4

## Bedford Park War Memorial
ST MICHAEL & ALL ANGELS CHURCH, THE AVENUE W4 1TT

GRADE: II  Erected c1919-20. Designed by Inigo Triggs. The war memorial commemorates the 44 men of Bedford Park who fell in the Great War 1914-18. It was paid for by public subscription. The original design for a memorial seat, which would "form a resting place, and also remind them of the resting place to which their dear ones had gone" was agreed at a public meeting in October 1917.
The structure is of Portland stone with neo-classical detailing, and takes the form of a tripartite seat with bold scrolled arm rests and ends. It is curved on plan, comprising three segmental curves. The high back bears a frieze with a series of inset slate panels inscribed with the names of the Fallen; these were installed in 1994 to replace the stolen bronze originals. The raised central section has a plaque inscribed:
TO THE GLORY OF GOD AND IN MEMORY OF MEN OF BEDFORD PARK WHO GAVE THEIR LIVES IN THE SERVICE OF THEIR COUNTRY IN THE GREAT WAR 1914-1918

# LONDON W8

## Kensington War Memorial
KENSINGTON HIGH STREET W8

GRADE: II A floriated style cross surmounting a stone pillar with a gothic design, column, pedestal and two-stepped base.

Four carved angels are placed in niches just beneath the cross. A draped female figure, symbolizing remembrance, stands at the foot of the column, right arm raised to a scroll with the dedication. The arms and motto of the Borough of Kensington are situated beneath the female figure.

On the banner above the draped figure:

AWAKE REMEMBRANCE OF THE VALIANT DEAD .

Below the former Metropolitan Borough of Kensington coat of arms:
QUID NOBIS ARDUI Latin approximately translates as 'what is hard for us'

On front of plinth:
IN MEMORY OF THE MEN OF KENSINGTON AND THOSE MEN SERVING IN KENSINGTON BATTALIONS WHO GAVE THEIR LIVES FOR KING AND COUNTRY IN THE GREAT WAR 1914-1918 1939-1945

# LONDON W12

## War Memorial
SHEPHERDS BUSH COMMON
W12

GRADE: II Winged bronze figure of peace on small hemisphere. Sword in hand, point downwards, laurel wreath in left. All standing on portland stone pedestal.

Inscription: IN GRATEFUL AND HONOURED MEMORY OF THE MEN OF THIS BOROUGH WHO FELL IN THE GREAT WAR 1914-1918
IN THE SIGHT OF THE UNWISE THEY SEEM TO DIE YET, IS THEIR HOPE FULL OF IMMORTALITY.

On a second plaque, below the first:
ALSO OF THOSE WHO GAVE THEIR LIVES IN THE SECOND WORLD WAR 1939-1945

## Medical Men and Women of the British Empire and Commonwealth
BMA TAVISTOCK SQUARE WC1

GRADE II  The memorial gates by Sir Edwin Lutyens were erected in 1925 in memory of the 574 BMA members who gave their lives in the First World War. They enclose the Court of Honour in which stands the memorial to the Medical Men and Women of the British Empire and Commonwealth who gave their lives in the Second World War. A circular stone fountain and four statues on pedestals of Sacrifice, Cure, Prevention, and Aspiration designed in 1954 by sculptor James Woodford. Inscription on fountain: IN MEMORIAM 1939-1945. Bronze plaque: IN HONOUR OF THE MEDICAL MEN AND WOMEN OF THE BRITISH EMPIRE AND COMMONWEALTH OF NATIONS WHO GAVE THEIR LIVES IN THE SECOND WORLD WAR. On a shield on the gates: FAITHFUL HATH BEEN YOUR WARFARE on reverse: MEMORY AND PRAISE. On a plaque: THE GATES OF REMEMBRANCE

# Rangers 12th County of London Regiment
## CHENIES STREET WC1

GRADE: II The 12th County of London Regiment ('the Rangers') war memorial. C.1920. Designer unknown.

Portland stone pylon with the regimental cap badge in bronze on the front; sandstone base.

Front inscription reads:
THE RANGERS 12TH COUNTY OF LONDON REGT 1914-1919 REMEMBER WITH GRATITUDE THE TRUE AND FAITHFUL MEN WHO IN THE GREAT WAR WENT FORTH FOR GOD AND THE RIGHT THE MEMORY OF THOSE WHO RETURNED NOT AGAIN IS HEREBY PERPETUATED TO BE HONOURED FOR EVERMORE

On the rear is the inscription:
TO THE MEMORY OF 1193 RANGERS WHO DIED FOR THE EMPIRE.

On each side is a list of First World War battles in which the regiment fought. Lower down on the front of the memorial are added inscriptions dating from after the Second World War: 'K.R.R.C. 1939-1945. Greece 1941 Crete Western Desert 1941. Veve, Proasteion, Canea. Retimo, Middle East 1941, Gazala. Retma, Bir Hacheim. Fuka Airfield North Africa 1942. Ruweisat. Defence of Alamein.

A Neoclassical pylon with an imposing list of engagements fought in by this rifle regiment.

## Belgian Monument to the British Nation

VICTORIA EMBANKMENT WC2

GRADE: II* This memorial was a tribute to Great Britain from the people of Belgium, in recognition of the welcome extended to refugees seeking refuge from the German invasion of Belgium in August 1914. This invasion led directly to Britain's entry into the First World War.
The memorial was unveiled by Princess Clementine of Belgium on 12 October 1920: the fifth anniversary of the execution in Brussels of Nurse Edith Cavell. A parallel memorial in Brussels, sculpted by Charles Sargeant Jagger, was unveiled in 1923.
Sculpture by Victor Rousseau, then a refugee in London; architectural setting by Sir Reginald Blomfield RA. The memorial consists of a bronze figural group set on a rectangular stone base. The group depicts a mother, drapery-clad and with an elongated neck, urging two garland-bearing children forward. According to the sculptor, "I designed the group representing Belgium as a woman draped in mourning, in the act of telling her children that Belgians will never forget their debt of gratitude to Great Britain. The garlands and other floral offerings borne by the children are symbolical of the wealth of the nine Belgian provinces. As for the children themselves, the lad and the little girl are designed to typify the spirit of youth and the confidence in the future, which is the most marked characteristic of the Belgian nation".
The group stands on a broad paved area, reached via four steps. Behind it is a stone screen, classical in design, with a taller central section flanked with curved wings: on the left is a relief carving depicting Justice, shown holding the 1837 Treaty of London which guaranteed Belgian neutrality, and matched on the right with one of Honour, represented as St George. At the top of the inset panels to the wings are relief carvings of the provinces of Belgium.
Inscription under the central sculptural group:
TO THE BRITISH NATION FROM THE GRATEFUL PEOPLE OF BELGIUM 1914 - 1918.

# LONDON WC2

## The Civil Service Rifles War Memorial
RIVERSIDE TERRACE, SOMERSET HOUSE, STRAND, WC2

GRADE: II* 1924 Memorial by architect Sir Edwin Landseer Lutyens. Commemorating the 1,240 servicemen who fell during the First World War. The Civil Service Rifles known as the 15th (County of London) Battalion, the London Regiment (Prince of Wales Own Civil Service Rifles) was raised from the members of the Civil Service, for which Somerset House had originally been built. The memorial, includes a roll of honour placed inside the column. The flags either side of the central column, which were originally executed in copper, have been replaced with carved stone. Cubical base with pillar surmounted by an urn and ornamented with laurel wreaths. Pillar has the King's and regimental colors on opposite sides.

Inscription (North face): THIS COLUMN WAS ERECTED BY THE 15TH COUNTY OF LONDON BATTALION THE LONDON REGIMENT PRINCE OF WALES OWN CIVIL SERVICE RIFLES
(South face): IN MEMORY OF THE 1240 WHO FELL WHILE SERVING WITH THE REGIMENT IN THE GREAT WAR THEIR NAMES ARE RECORDED ON A SCROLL PLACED WITHIN THIS COLUMN ALSO IN MEMORY OF MEMBERS OF THE CIVIL SERVICE CADET BATTALION
(On base): FESTUBERT LOOS SOMME 1918 COURCHFLETTE DOIRN 1917 LYS KEMMEL GAZA NEBISAMIWIL JERUSALEM ST QUENTIN ALBERT 1918 ANCRE 1918 BAPAUME 1918 SELLE TRANSLOY YPRES 1917 1918 MESSINES 1917 1918 CAMBRAI 1917

# LONDON WC2

## Edith Cavell Memorial
ST MARTIN'S PLACE WC2

GRADE: I 1920 memorial, Carrara marble statue, Cornish grey granite by Sir George Frampton RA commemorates one of the most famous civilian casualties of the First World War, and stands out as a rare war memorial to an individual woman.

Edith Cavell (1865-1915) was a British nurse from Norfolk. She was matron at Berkendael Medical Institute in Brussels when the First World War broke out in 1914. In addition to nursing soldiers from both sides without distinction, she assisted some 200 Allied soldiers escape from German-occupied Belgium. She was arrested in August 1915, court-martialled, found guilty of treason, and shot by a German firing squad on 12 October 1915. Her story was used in British propaganda as an example of German barbarism. Her remains were initially buried in Belgium, but returned to Britain after the war in 1919 for a state funeral at Westminster Abbey before she was finally buried at Norwich Cathedral.

Nurse Cavell's statue, in the nurse's uniform she wore to face the firing squad, stands on a two-stage plinth inscribed BRUSSELS DAWN OCTOBER 12th 1915: beneath, in smaller letters, is added PATRIOTISM IS NOT ENOUGH I MUST HAVE NO HATRED OR BITTERNESS TOWARDS ANYONE those were her words of forgiveness to an Anglican chaplain who was permitted to give her Holy Communion on the night before her execution. These words were initially left off, and added in 1924 at the request of the National Council of Women.

Behind is a tall pylon, inscribed on each face, at frieze height, HUMANITY / SACRIFICE / DEVOTION / FORTITUDE.

On the rear of the memorial is a relief of a lion, standing triumphant over a serpent: this symbolized the Britain's overcoming envy, malice, spite and treachery. Below this is a hammer-beaten panel, showing the granite in its roughest state. The upper section is cruciform in shape, and comprises a sculptural group of a woman and infant, depicting Humanity: over the folds of her skirt is the Geneva cross.

To the front of the upper shaft, between wreaths, is the inscription FOR KING AND COUNTRY.

# LONDON WC2

## Imperial Camel Corps Memorial
VICTORIA EMBANKMENT GARDENS WC2

GRADE: II Memorial. 1921 by Cecil Brown. Bronze statuette of figure mounted on camel set on Portland stone pedestal with bronze bas-relief.

First raised in 1916, the Imperial Camel Corps was a camel-mounted infantry force operating in the Middle Eastern and African deserts. The Corps played an integral role in several First World War desert campaigns, including Palestine and Sinai.

The Corps had a small start, with the first companies consisting of Australian troops returning from the Gallipoli campaign. Over time, it grew to four battalions and was made up of Australian, New Zealand and British troops. Additional soldiers from the Hong Kong and Singapore Mountain Battery were also attached to the Corps.

At its height the Corps, which fought in numerous campaigns throughout the Middle East, comprised of 4,150 men and 4,800 camels. Thanks to their humped steeds, the soldiers were able to travel long distances across remote desert terrain, carrying machine guns, mountain artillery and medical support. 346 troops from the Imperial Camel Corps lost their lives.

Inscription : TO THE GLORIOUS AND IMMORTAL MEMORY OF THE OFFICERS, NCO's AND MEN OF THE IMPERIAL CAMEL CORPS, BRITISH, AUSTRALIAN, NEW ZEALAND, INDIAN, WHO FELL IN ACTION OR DIED OF WOUNDS AND DISEASE IN EGYPT, SINAI AND PALESTINE, 1916 -1917-1918.

The south face of the stone plinth is inscribed: Engagements 1916: Romani, Baharia, Mazar, Dakhla, Maghara, El. Arish, Maghdaba 1917: Rafa, Hassana, Gaza 1, Gaza 2, Sana Redoubt, Beersheba, Bir Khu Weilfe, Hill 265 1918: Amman, Jordan Valley, Mudawar (Hedjaz)

A bronze plaque on the east face lists those from the Australian Contingent who fell (191). One on the west face lists those from the British (106), the New Zealand (41) and the Indian (9) Contingents.

## Lincoln's Inn (Inns of Court Regiment) War Memorial
NEWMANS ROW, LINCOLNS INN WC2

GRADE: II War memorial. 1921 to the fallen of Lincoln's Inn.
The Portland stone memorial comprises a central pylon with a curved screen incorporating seats to either side, terminating with piers at each end. The ensemble is about 46 feet (14 m) long and stands on a stone base with three steps.
Carved along the top of the monument: HOSPITIUM SOCIIS SANGUINEM PRO PATRIA LARGITIS FILIIS PARENTES Translates from the Latin, as: Offer your solidarity in honour of the allied sons who generously gave their blood for their country.
Brass plaques on the inside face of each pier record the names of the fallen from the First World War, listing 35 people in total. A bronze plaque on the central pylon listing 66 further names of the fallen from the First World War, in two columns. Later, a second plaque was added listing another 29 names from the Second World War, including Prince George, Duke of Kent.
Other war memorials in Lincoln's inn include a table, a book of remembrance, a plaque in the chapel, and a memorial to a Zeppelin air raid in 1915.

# BARKING and DAGENHAM

## Barking Park War Memorial
BARKING PARK, LONGBRIDGE ROAD IG11 8QX

GRADE: II   War memorial in remembrance of the men of Barking lost in the First and Second World Wars. Unveiled in 1922. Designed by local architect C J Dawson FRIBA. The memorial stands in the rond point of a path in the North-West part of Barking Park. It comprises a three-stepped flagstone pavement with a centrally positioned pylon and curved, flanking, walls. The 3m tall pylon features a centrally positioned stone laurel wreath carved in relief which is flanked by the inscribed and gilt dates 1914 1918.

A plaque below the wreath and reads IN GRATITUDE TO ALL WHO SERVED, AND IN HONOUR OF THE MEN OF BARKING WHO FELL IN THE GREAT WAR THEY GAVE THEMSELVES FOR FREEDOM'S CAUSE THEIR MEMORY NEVER DIES 1939-1945 . Inscribed underneath 1939-1945.

The 3m tall flanking walls, bear carved and gilt inscriptions. The walls carry 14 bronze name plaques.

Inscription on the rear of the pylon  THIS MAST WITH FLAGS WAS PRESENTED TO THE TOWN OF BARKING BY ARTHUR W. SMITH, ESQ., ON THE CONCLUSION OF PEACE AS A TOKEN OF REMEMBRANCE OF THOSE OF OUR TOWN WHO SERVED IN HIS MAJESTY'S FORCES DURING THE GREAT WAR OF 1914-18 OF WHOM MANY WERE WOUNDED AND OTHERS GAVE THEIR LIVES FOR KING AND COUNTRY BEING THE MEANS OF SAVING OUR NATION AND EMPIRE, PROTECTING US AND OUR HOMES AND STANDING FOR JUSTICE AND RIGHTEOUSNESS IN THE WORLD.  JULY 19 1919

This inscription refers to a flagpole on the central pylon, which was part of the original design but is now missing.

# BARNET

## New Barnet (East Barnet Valley) War Memorial
STATION ROAD, NEW BARNET EN5

GRADE: II  Erected 1921, designed by Newbury Abbot Trent ARA

The New Barnet (East Barnet Valley) War Memorial stands on a triangular island in the centre of the town; it was created as a memorial to the men of the East Barnet Valley who fell during the First World War.

The memorial comprises a four-sided 5.18m tall obelisk of Portland stone, surmounted by a bronze allegorical 'winged victory' figure holding a palm leaf, standing on a globe supported by four fish, which adds a further 2.43m to the height of the monument. The obelisk has a simple stylised base and is mounted on a tall pedestal with recessed corners and a plain plinth, set on a stepped Portland stone podium, raised on a concrete base.

A seated lion beneath a rising sun is carved in relief at the base of the western side of the column; incised on a stone panel at the lion's feet are the words 'AT THE GOING DOWN OF THE SUN AND IN THE MORNING WE WILL REMEMBER THEM'. The base of the column on the reverse side is carved 1914 - 1918, and 1939 - 1945 is carved on the plinth.

The surnames and initials of the 278 fallen of the First World War are carved into slate panels attached on all four sides of the pedestal. Unusually, a woman's name appears on the memorial – Amy Alice Victoria Goldsmith. She died on 5th March 1919 aged 32 years, while serving as a staff nurse of the Territorial Force Nursing Service attached to the 57th General Hospital, Marseilles. An additional panel recording the 136 men killed during the Second World War has been placed at the foot of the podium on the eastern side of the memorial.

# BEXLEY

## Bexley War Memorial
Corner HURST ROAD and
PARKHILL ROAD
BEXLEY  DA5 1HT

---

1919 memorial. Two stepped octagonal base surmounted by plinth, and cross. Inscription carved on the sides of the plinth. Bronze sword placed on the front face of the cross.
Inscription  IN PROUD AND LOVING MEMORY OF THE BEXLEY MEN WHO GAVE THEIR LIVES FOR THEIR KING AND COUNTRY IN THE GREAT WARS 1914-1918
LIVE THOU FOR ENGLAND WE FOR ENGLAND DIED
Other faces: (Names)

# BROMLEY

## Bromley War Memorial
MARTINS HILL PARK, BROMLEY BR2 0XH

GRADE: II* Memorial, 1922 by Sydney March. Bronze allegorical figures on three sides of obelisk with a bronze cartouche to the rear. The three figures in cast bronze represent Victory in the front centre, winged and holding aloft a wreath, Liberty on the left holding a torch and Peace on the right scattering flowers of remembrance from her lap. The Portland stone pedestal is 27 feet 6 inches high. The monument records the names of 769 soldiers from the area who died in World War I. It also lists the names of 476 soldiers and civilians who were killed during World War II.
Inscriptions: (Names of the fallen) ALSO REMEMBERED WITH GRATEFUL APPRECIATION THOSE WHO, SINCE THE SECOND WORLD WAR, HAVE GIVEN THEIR LIVES IN CONFLICTS AND PEACE-KEEPING MISSIONS THROUGHOUT THE WORLD
Plaque: THIS MEMORIAL IS DEDICATED TO THOSE OF OUR PEOPLE WHO LOST THEIR LIVES IN THE WAR OF 1914-1918 AND 1939-1945
On back: IN PROUD MEMORY OF MANY BRAVE MEN WHO WENT FORTH FROM THIS TOWN AND SERVED THEIR KING AND COUNTRY IN THE GREAT WAR 1914-1918 AND IN THAT SERVICE

# CROYDON

## Croydon Aerodrome Battle Of Britain Memorial
PURLEY WAY, CROYDON CR0 4RS

The airfield and airport site had both military and civil phases. It opened in 1916 and closed in 1955. Originally known as Beddington Aerodrome, the site was opened as a Home Defence base by the Royal Flying Corps during the First World War. It is said to have been the world's first international airport and was used for extensive passenger traffic in the 1920s and 1930s. During World War Two it was requisitioned by the Royal Air Force to be used as a satellite airfield, used by fighter aircraft. In 1940, during the Battle of Britain it was bombed by German aircraft.

The memorial erected in 1992 commemorates the use of the site during the Battle of Britain.

Bronze eagle resting on an obelisk and a base of three square steps. Buried under the monument is a time capsule containing historic items relating to the Battle of Britain and Croydon Airport.

Inscription in white lettering, crests of different squadrons :-
East side: FIGHTER COMMAND   South side: 501 SQUADRON; 605 SQUADRON; 607 SQUADRON, ALL AUXILIARY AIR FORCE   West side: 145 SQUADRON, RAF; 401 SQUADRON, ROYAL CANADIAN AIR FORCE   North side: 72 SQUADRON, RAF; 85 SQADRON, RAF; CXI FIGHTER SQUADRON, RAF

Inscription on the front of the pylon:
IN GOD WE TRUST THIS MEMORIAL IS IN TRIBUTE TO ALL CONNECTED WITH CROYDON AND ITS AERODROME WHO GAVE THEIR LIVES EITHER IN THE AIR OR ON THE GROUND DURING THE SECOND WORLD WAR 1939 - 1945
THIS MEMORIAL WAS UNVEILED BY AIR MARSHAL SIR WILLIAM WRATTEN KBE CB AFC FRAES, RAF ON SUNDAY 27TH OCTOBER 1991
NEVER IN THE FIELD OF HUMAN CONFLICT WAS SO MUCH OWED BY SO MANY TO SO FEW WSC

On the right face of the pylon:
REMEMBERED ALWAYS ALL CIVIL DEFENCE UNITS - TELEPHONE SERVICES - TRANSPORT - DOCTORS AND NURSING STAFF - POST & ALL THOSE WHO SUFFERED

On the left face of the pylon:
THEY GAVE US FREEDOM   ROYAL ARTILLERY - HON ARTILLERY COMPANY - QUEENS ROYAL REG - MIDDLESEX REG - TOWER HAMLETS RIFLES - 2ND LONDON RIFLES - W.A.A.F. - A.T.S. - A.T.A.

On the back:
THE POSSIBILTY OF DEFEAT NEVER EXISTED AMBULANCE - FIRE - POLICE - ROYAL OBSERVER CORPS- HOME GUARD- N.A.A.F.I. SALVATION ARMY

# CROYDON

## Croydon Cenotaph
KATHARINE STREET, CROYDON CR9 1ET

GRADE: II* First and Second World War memorial erected 1921, by James Burford and Paul Montford. Croydon Cenotaph was raised as permanent testament to the sacrifice made by the members of the local community who lost their lives in the First World War. The memorial is of particular note for the balance struck between military and domestic suffering and for the sculptural quality of the figures.

The memorial comprises a 9m high Portland stone pylon surmounted by a sarcophagus. A bronze cross flanked by the dates 1914 and 1918 sits at at the top of the pylon; the dates 1939 and 1945 were added subsequently.

The left statue represents a soldier of the East Surrey Regiment dressing a wound on his own arm. He is sat on his greatcoat, with his rifle behind him and a Mills bomb at his feet. His water bottle is in his lap, and his puttees are covered with sacking. The soldier is helmetless, and has a field dressing around his head.

The right statue shows a woman in civilian dress holding a child on her lap. She, too, is sat on a coat. Her right arm is stretched out towards the soldier, and is clutching a letter. Her face is also turned in the direction of the soldier, and her wedding ring is clearly visible, suggesting the three figures constitute a family.

The pylon is inscribed: AND IN MEMORY OF THOSE WHO LOST THEIR LIVES IN WARS AND CONFLICTS SINCE.
A TRIBUTE TO THE MEN AND WOMEN OF CROYDON WHO DIED AND SUFFERED.

The memorial is incorporated into the balustrade of the Town Hall.

# ENFIELD

### Enfield War Memorial — CHASE SIDE, ENFIELD EN2 6SG

GRADE: II  War memorial. 1921. Portland stone. The memorial comprises a tall, tapering pedestal placed over a stepped base, set within a paved area with twelve stone posts, lined with chains. The upper stage of the pedestal has fluted sides with a single leaf per end: on the fronts are wreaths set against a plain panel. Above the heavy cornice is a tapering sarcophagus on a moulded base: this has two ring handles per main side, and a scrolled cover with volutes at the top.
The front of the pedestal is inscribed OUR GLORIOUS DEAD.
On the sides are the dates 1914 - 1919 and 1939 - 1945.
The National Inventory of War Memorials reports that a 'cenotaph in Enfield' was unveiled by Lt-Gen Sir Francis Lloyd on 30 October 1921. It contained a capsule, within which were placed copies of The Times, The Enfield Gazette and Observer, an autographed list of members of the Enfield Patriots' Committee, and coins of the realm.

# HARROW

Harrow on the Hill War Memorial        GROVE HILL, HA1 3AQ

GRADE: II   War Memorial 1921. William Douglas Caroe architect. Portland stone. Free Gothic style, in the form of a wayside calvary cross. Octagonal base with four steps, inscribed with the names of the dead. Plinth with set-back corners; fielded panels to each face, the central one with raised gilded lettering reading HARROW ON THE HILL TOWN MEMORIAL. Above is an octagonal frieze with inscription in Lombardic script opening TO THE GLORIOUS MEMORY; lower register embellished with ball-flower ornament. Tapering cross on base above, with coped cover to top, cusped supports to transverse arms below.

# HARROW

## Harrow School War Memorial Building and Memorial Shrine
GROVE HILL, HARROW HA1 3HL

GRADE: II* 1921-6 memorial building, by Sir Herbert Baker. Two-storeys, with tall first floor of 3 large rooms.

The War Memorial was opened to commemorate the 2917 Harrovians who served in the First World War, 690 of whom were injured and 644 were killed.

The shrine was completed by 1923 and open to visits ahead of construction of the wider building and staircase.

The outstanding decoration of the room above the Shrine was funded by Lady Fitch in memory of her son, Alexander Fitch. She required the inclusion of a symbolic light that may never be extinguished in the Alex Fitch Room, a flame in honour of the fallen whose memory lives on and as a fine example of a substantial memorial.

The tripartite, dome-vaulted stone shrine contains an ashlar cenotaph (sarcophagus), with ornate sword carved on top, with dedicatory inscription IN MEMORY OF THE SONS OF HARROW WHO DIED IN THE GREAT WAR 1914-1919, and carved wreaths on flanking ends. The walls of the loggia contain panels inscribed with the names of the fallen, each surmounted by a gilded inscription, reading: BE THOU STRONG AND OF GOOD COURAGE BE NOT AFRAID NEITHER BE THOU DISMAYED BE THOU FAITHFUL UNTO DEATH AND I WILL GIVE THEE A CROWN OF LIFE REMEMBER THOSE WHO DIED FOR FREEDOM AND HONOUR AND SEE YOU TO IT THAT THEY SHALL NOT BE FORGOTTEN.

# HAVERING

## Rainham War Memorial
BROADWAY, RAINHAM RM13 9YW

---

GRADE: II War Memorial clock tower. 1920 by Mr Vinton, builder. Red Belgian brick, Portland and cast stone dressings.
Six sided brick short tower with a clock at the top of three sides with an alcove beneath and stone blocks inscribed 'LEST WE FORGET'. Other three sides have white stone tablets attached with incription and names. Upper parapet with balustrade. New base added for WW2 names.
Inscription on tablet side 1: 1914-1919 REMEMBER WITH THANKSGIVING THE TRUE AND FAITHFUL MEN WHO IN THESE YEARS OF WAR WENT FORTH FROM THIS PLACE FOR GOD AND THE RIGHT THE NAMES OF THOSE WHO RETURNED NOT AGAIN ARE HERE INSCRIBED TO BE HONOURED FOR EVERMORE. 1939-1945. (NAMES)
Tablet side 2: (NAMES) TO THE 54 MEN, WOMEN AND CHILDREN OF THIS TOWN WHO WERE KILLED BY ENEMY ACTION 1939-1945.
Tablet side 3: (NAMES) BASE: (NAMES)

# HILLINGDON

## Harefield War Memorial
HAREFIELD VILLAGE GREEN, BREAKSPEAR ROAD NORTH, HAREFIELD UB9 6PL

GRADE: II  The memorial, commemorating those from the village of Harefield who fell in the First World War, was designed by the architect Frederic Herbert Mansford, and dedicated in 1921. The names of the fallen from the Second World War were added in 1948.
In 2014, two engraved paving slabs were added at the foot of the memorial commemorating two First World War recipients of the Victoria Cross who were born in the village, Private Cecil John Kinross and Private Robert Edward Ryder. These include depictions of the Victoria Cross, names of the regiments and the dates the actions for which the award was made took place. The memorial takes the form of a 10m high obelisk, standing on a plinth with a two-tiered base. Each face of the plinth is adorned with a laurel leaf swag. Inscription on one plinth 'TO THE GLORIOUS DEAD' with the other three sides bearing the names of the 79 fallen. The names of the 34 fallen of the Second World War are inscribed on the base of the obelisk itself.
The memorial is surrounded by a rectangular area of stone paving slabs with four panels of pebble cobbles and a flight of six stone steps descending the pond bank. The steps are flanked at the top by a pair of low stone piers.

# HILLINGDON

## The Polish War Memorial
JUNCTION WITH WESTERN AVENUE, WEST END ROAD, RUISLIP HA4 6QX

GRADE: II  Unveiled in 1948, designed by Mieczyslaw Lubelski, who had been interned in a forced labour camp during the war. Portland stone shaft on plinth surmounted by a bronze eagle, the symbol of the Polish Air Force. Set behind a pool with fountain. Portland stone gate piers with cast iron railings to front, semi-circular area to rear lined with inscription panels of grey granite, bearing the names of Polish fliers killed in action, together with the crests of the Polish RAF squadrons they served with. The front of the shaft bears the dates 1940 1945, and lists the RAF squadrons formed from Polish fliers as well as a list of battle honours. The front of the plinth reads 'TO THE MEMORY OF FALLEN POLISH AIRMEN' and 'POLECLYM LOTNIKOM POLSKIM'; the rear has the inscription 'I HAVE FOUGHT A GOOD FIGHT. I HAVE FINISHED MY COURSE. I HAVE KEPT THE FAITH (II Timothy iv, 7)'.
Plaque on right: THIS MEMORIAL COMMEMORATES THE 2165 POLISH AIRMEN WHO LOST THEIR LIVES IN WORLD WAR II FIGHTING ALONGSIDE THE WESTERN ALLIES THE POLISH AIR FORCE IN GREAT BRITAIN WAS FORMED IN 1940 FROM

AIRMEN WHO AFTER THE FALL OF POLAND IN 1939 HAD ESCAPED TO FRANCE WHERE THEY FOUGHT UNTIL ITS COLLAPSE, AND FROM POLES LIVING IN THE USA, CANADA, ARGENTINA AND OTHER COUNTRIES THEIR RANKS WERE INCREASED BY POLES RELEASED FROM THE SOVIET LABOUR CAMPS AND SIBERIAN EXILE. IN ALL, SOME 17,000 MEN AND WOMEN SERVED IN THE POLISH AIR FORCE, WHICH COMPRISED 16 OPERATIONAL FLYING SQUADRONS THIS MEMORIAL WAS ERECTED IN 1948 AND SUBSTANTIALLY RESTORED IN 1996 FROM PUBLIC DONATIONS. IT IS ADJACENT TO THE ROYAL AIR FORCE STATION NORTHOLT, WHICH WAS THE MAIN BASE FOR THE POLISH FIGHTER SQUADRONS DURING THE BATTLE OF BRITAIN

This monument was erected to mark the winding-up of the 14 RAF squadrons manned by Polish airmen, and their contribution to the allied victory. Of the 17,000 persons who served, over 2,000 were killed. It is among the earliest of memorials erected to Second World War airmen.

## Polish War Memorial Remembrance Garden
JUNCTION WESTERN AVENUE, WEST END ROAD, RUISLIP HA4 6QX

*Below:* An information panel in the Remembrance Garden

# Polish War Memorial Remembrance Garden
## This memorial garden is dedicated with grateful thanks to the Polish Air Force by the London Borough of Hillingdon

On the 1 September 1939, Poland was invaded by Germany and on the 17 September by Russia. Polish aircraft were out-classed by the latest German designs, but the Luftwaffe still lost 285 aircraft, 126 credited to air to air combat. With the defeat of Poland inevitable, most members of the Polish Air Force evacuated through Romania to France where they flew with the French Air Force, and were credited with a further 60 Luftwaffe aircraft.

By June 1940 some 6,000 members of the Polish Air Force had re-formed in Great Britain. The initial RAF scepticism changed to admiration for the skills and unstinting dedication of pilots and ground crew alike. Polish airmen reinforced Fighter Command in the critical weeks from mid-August to mid-September when the Battle of Britain hung in the balance. 145 Polish pilots, some five per cent of Fighter Command's strength, claimed 203 German aircraft destroyed for the loss of 29 killed. This represents seven and a half per cent of the total number of Allied victories, or 1.4 enemy aircraft for every Pole engaged. At the same time the two Polish squadrons suffered losses 70 per cent lower than most RAF units.

On the 15 September, celebrated in the United Kingdom as 'Battle of Britain Day', one in five of the pilots in action was Polish. At the end of the 16-week campaign, the top-scoring Fighter Command unit was 303 Polish Squadron, which in only six weeks was credited with 126 enemy aircraft. Arguably the most successful individual pilot – with 17 victories – was Sergeant Josef František, a Czech member of 303 Squadron.

Eventually, the Polish Air Force amounted to some 20,000 personnel, formed into 15 squadrons plus two additional special flights attached to British units, and supported by Polish training schools, engineers and administration. Individual Polish pilots also flew with RAF and USAF squadrons. At the end of the war Poland was handed over by the Allies to the control of the same Soviet Union which had invaded her in 1939. Polish Armed Forces were excluded from the 1946 Victory Parade and disbanded. The Polish Government in Exile established during the war years remained in Great Britain until Poland regained sovereignty in 1990.

In 1945 the Polish Air Force Association (PAFA) was founded to look after the welfare of resettled Polish airmen in this country. The Polish sculptor Mieczysław Lubelski was commissioned to design a Memorial to be engraved with the names of 1,241 aircrew killed in operational flights. The Memorial was unveiled on 2 November 1948, All Souls' Day, by Lord Tedder, Chief of the Air Staff, following a speech by Viscount Portal of Hungerford. The Memorial was re-dedicated on 6 September 1996 with the addition of another 659 names who died on active service. The Memorial and its grounds are maintained by the London Borough of Hillingdon.

# HOUNSLOW

## Heston War Memorial
NEW HESTON ROAD
HOUNSLOW TW5 0LH

---

GRADE: II 1918 by Arthur G. Walker. Portland stone. Statue of a private soldier in full marching kit, standing at ease. Square pedestal over a three stage stepped base, with lists of names of the fallen and reliefs of naval activity on each side. Matching posts and chains surround the memorial.

Front inscription: IN HONOUR OF THE MEN OF THIS VILLAGE WHO FELL IN THE GREAT WAR 1914-1918.

A later inscription was added to the base, reading REMEMBER ALSO THE MEN AND WOMEN OF HESTON WHO GAVE THEIR LIVES IN THE SECOND WORLD WAR 1939-1945.

The memorial was unveiled on June 1st 1918, several months before the Armistice. The memorial originally stood on a shallow earthen mound; the present stepped base was formed after 1945.

# KINGSTON UPON THAMES

## Kingston upon Thames WW1 and WW2 Memorial
MEMORIAL GARDEN,
UNION STREET,
KINGSTON UPON THAMES
KT1 1RP

GRADE: II* First World War memorial by Richard Goulden, unveiled on 11 November 1923, with Second World War additions. The memorial stands within the gated memorial gardens on the site of a former burial ground. The sculpture depicts the male striding forward, with left arm raised to hold a flaming crucifix, and right arm lowered to vanquish a serpent that he tramples while protecting two small children from the beast and from thorns. These children shelter by his right side. One stands close to him, looking up at his face, the other crouches behind him for safety.

Around the base of the bronze sculpture is inscribed: AT THE GOING DOWN OF THE SUN AND IN THE MORNING WE WILL REMEMBER THEM (from Laurence Binyon's 1914 poem For the Fallen).

At the front of pedestal, beneath the sculpture, is inscribed: IN HONOUR OF THE MEN OF THIS TOWN WHO GAVE THEIR LIVES IN THE GREAT WARS 1914 – 1919 / 1939 – 1945.

The granite pedestal carries the principal inscription in applied bronze. The lower part of this, continuing onto the low flanking walls, carries bronze relief panels bearing 624 First World War names. The principal inscription now includes a dedication to the Second World War but no names were added.

## Bromhead Memorial
RICHMOND & EAST SHEEN CEMETERY, LOWER GROVE ROAD, TW10 6HW

GRADE: II 1957 by Cecil Thomas. Memorial to servicemen who were patients at the Royal Star and Garter Home and who were not otherwise commemorated. The home in Richmond was built on a site granted by Queen Mary for the establishment of a home to care for invalided ex-servicemen; the home was originally established in the former Star and Garter Hotel. The Star and Garter Society became an independent charity in 1922 and shortly thereafter decided that the hotel was unsuitable for the needs of the residents. It was demolished, and the purpose-built home was built on the same site. The society operated the home from that site until 2013, when it moved to new premises.

The Cemetery contains two sections dedicated to former residents of the Star and Garter Home, one of which is marked by the Bromhead Memorial. The memorial was commissioned as a gift from the Bromhead family in the name of Lieutenant Colonel Alfred Bromhead—who served as a governor of the Star and Garter home—and his wife Margaret, who was also a governor and the home's matron. The memorial is in the form of a triptych set on a base of three steps. The central panel is inscribed: THIS MONUMENT IS ERECTED IN MEMORY OF THOSE PATIENTS WHO HAVE DIED IN THE STAR AND GARTER HOME FOR DISABLED SAILORS SOLDIERS AND AIRMEN WHO ARE NOT OTHERWISE COMMEMORATED AND WHOSE NAMES ARE INSCRIBED HEREON AND IN THE BOOK AT THE HOME

Each panel is inscribed with a roll of honour in chronological sequence from 1928 to 1958. The names continue on the reverse of the memorial, spanning the years 1970-1977. Set forward from the rear wall is a lower spine wall. It is inscribed on both faces, covering the years 1961-66 to the left and 1966-70 to the right. To the front is a seated, sentinel lion. The riser of the step to the front of the memorial is inscribed: Given by Lt Col AC Bromhead CBE JP Chairman of the House Committee of Governors 1915-1956.

Commemorative slabs inscribed: In most loving memory of the same Lt Col Alfred Claude Bromhead CBE JP Who died 5th March 1963 aged 86 at Petersham Beloved husband and father His ashes lie here His life and devotion to family Was an example and inspiration to many and In loving memory of his wife Margaret Eileen Bromhead A former matron and governor Of the Star and Garter Home Who died 18th October 1978 Aged 72

# RICHMOND UPON THAMES

## South African War Memorial
RICHMOND & EAST SHEEN CEMETERY, LOWER GROVE ROAD, RICHMOND TW10 6HP

GRADE: II Monument to the fallen of the First World War from South Africa.

Designed by architect Sir Edwin Lutyens, the memorial is in the form of a cenotaph, similar to that on Whitehall, also by Lutyens. It was commissioned by the South African Hospital and Comforts Fund Committee to commemorate the 39 South African soldiers who died of their wounds at a military hospital in Richmond Park during the First World War. The memorial was unveiled in 1921 and was the focus of pilgrimages from South Africa through the 1920s and 1930s. The memorial, which overlooks the graves, is inscribed in both English and Dutch.

The outward face is inscribed: UNION IS STRENGTH OUR GLORIOUS DEAD Below is an inscribed cross.

The inner face, overlooking the group of graves, is inscribed in Dutch: EENGRAGHT MAAKT MACHT   ONZEN GEVALLENEN HELDEN

In the apex of each face is the head of a springbok, in low relief, the national symbol of South Africa.

The side elevations have a stylised stone wreath at the base and are inscribed to north and south respectively with the dates MCM XIV and MCM XIX.

# RICHMOND UPON THAMES

## The Cross of Sacrifice
RICHMOND & EAST SHEEN CEMETERY,
LOWER GROVE ROAD,
RICHMOND TW10 6HP

---

The Cross of Sacrifice is a Commonwealth war memorial designed in 1918 by Sir Reginald Blomfield for the Imperial War Graves Commission (now the Commonwealth War Graves Commission).
It is present in Commonwealth war cemeteries containing 40 or more graves.
Its shape is an elongated Latin cross with proportions more typical of the Celtic cross, with the shaft and crossarm octagonal in section. It ranges in height from 18 to 24 feet (5.5 to 7.3 m). A bronze longsword, blade down, is affixed to the front of the cross (and sometimes to the back as well). It is usually mounted on an octagonal base. It may be freestanding or incorporated into other cemetery features.
The Cross of Sacrifice is widely praised, widely imitated, and the archetypal British war memorial. It is the most imitated of Commonwealth war memorials, and duplicates and imitations have been used around the world.
Inscription on the base:
THIS CROSS OF SACRIFICE IS ONE IN DESIGN AND INTENTION WITH THOSE WHICH HAVE BEEN SET UP IN FRANCE AND BELGIUM AND OTHER PLACES THROUGHOUT THE WORLD WHERE OUR DEAD OF THE GREAT WAR ARE LAID TO REST
THEIR NAME LIVETH FOR EVERMORE

# SUTTON

## Sutton War Memorial
MANOR PARK, SUTTON SM1 4BF

GRADE: II First World War memorial, designed by J S W Burmester and unveiled 1921, with Second World War additions. It carries the names of 518 men who fell in the war. In addition, the memorial is also dedicated to one woman, Eliza Bailey, aged 22, from Sutton who lost her life during the war. She was killed in an accident at the munitions factory based at Brocks firework factory in Gander Green Lane. The memorial comprises a Latin cross with octagonal cross arms embellished with carved details in the corners of the cross arms and surmounting an octagonal tapering shaft with carved collar and base. At the base of the shaft on each corner spur of the plinth is a carved angel and in between are the carved emblems of the Army, Navy and the Air Force. The sides of the plinth have recessed stone panels carved with arched surrounds and twelve bronze panels, three facing each way, bear the names of the fallen.

Inscription on a bronze panel which reads: THIS SIGN OF THE GREAT SACRIFICE IS RAISED IN HONOUR OF OUR HEROIC DEAD WHO GAVE THEIR LIVES FOR ENGLAND IN THE GREAT WAR THEIR NAME LIVETH FOR EVERMORE.

On the front face is an inscription : AND IN MEMORY OF THOSE MEN AND WOMEN OF SUTTON WHO GAVE THEIR LIVES IN DEFENCE OF FREEDOM IN THE WORLD WAR 1939 – 1945.

Another panel below reads: THE PEOPLE OF SUTTON ERECTED THIS MONUMENT AND DEDICATED THE FOUR ACRES OF GROUND SURROUNDING IT TO THE USE OF THE PUBLIC FOR EVER. JUNE 1921.

# ALPHABETICAL INDEX

6th Dragoon Guards (The Carabiniers) 77
7th July Memorial 81
22nd Battalion, The London Regiment 47
24th East Surrey Division 80
African and Caribbean War Memorial 76
Animals in War Memorial 82
Australian War Memorial 48
Bali Bombings Memorial 49
Barking Park War Memorial 105
Battle of Britain Monument 50
Bedford Park War Memorial 95
Belgian Monument to the British Nation 100
Bexley War Memorial 107
Bromhead Memorial 120
Bromley War Memorial 108
Boadicea/ Boudica 52
Boer War Memorial 35
Cadiz Memorial 53
Canadian Memorial 54
Cavalry of the Empire Memorial 84
Cenotaph 55
Children of Upper North Street School 15
Chindit Memorial 56
Chingford War Memorial 12
City and County of London Troops 22
Civilian Deaths of East London 9
Civil Service Rifles War Memorial 101
Combined Forces Memorial 57
Commonwealth Memorial Gates 58
Communist Victims/Twelve Responses to Tragedy 79
Crimea and Indian Mutiny 59
Cross of Sacrifice 122
Croydon Aerodrome Battle of Britain Memorial 109
Croydon Cenotaph 110
Eagle Squadrons Memorial 85
East Ham War Memorial 13
Edith Cavell Memorial 102
Enfield War Memorial 111
Falklands Merchant Seafarers 24
Fleet Air Arm Memorial 60
Following the Leader 46
Fulham War Memorial 78
Fulham (All Saints) War Memorial 78
Gas Workers Memorial 11
Great Eastern Railway War Memorial 20

Great Western Railway War Memorial 92
The Guards Memorial 61
The Guards Crimean War Memorial 62
Gurkha Memorial 63
Harefield War Memorial 115
Harrow on the Hill War Memorial 112
Harrow School War Memorial Building & Shrine 113
Heston War Memorial 118
Hornsey War Memorial 36
Imperial Camel Corps 103
International Brigade Spanish Civil War 41
Iraq and Afghanistan Memorial 64
Islington Green War Memorial 33
Katyn Massacre Memorial 94
Kensington War Memorial 96
Kindertransport Sculpture 21
Kingston upon Thames WW1 & WW2 Memorial 119
Korean War Memorial 65
La Delivrance 34
Lancaster Gate Memorial Cross 93
Lincolns Inn (Inns of Court Regiment) Memorial 104
London & North Western Railway War Memorial 39
Machine Gun Corps 86
Malta War Memorial 25
Marylebone War Memorial 87
Medical Men and Women 98
Men Of Finchley 37
Mercantile Marine First World War 26
Merchant Seamens Second World War 28
National Firefighters Memorial 31
National Submariners' War Memorial 32
New Barnet (East Barnet Valley) War Memorial 106
New Zealand War Memorial 88
Polish War Memorial 116
Postal Workers War Memorial 17
Prisoners of War & Concentration Camps 40
Prudential War Memorial 18
RAF Bomber Command 90
Rainham War Memorial 114
Rangers 12th County of London Regiment 99
Rifle Brigade War Memorial 66
Royal Air Force Memorial 67
Royal Artillery Memorial 68
Royal Artillery Memorial - Boer War 70
Royal Fusiliers War Memorial 19

Royal Marines National Memorial  71
Royal Naval Division Memorial  72
St John at Hackney War Memorial  14
St Michael Cornhill War Memorial  29
St Saviours Southwark War Memorial  42
Shepherds Bush War Memorial  97
South African War Memorial  121
Soviet War Memorial  43
Stairway to Heaven  10
Sutton War Memorial  123
Unknown Warrior  74
Victims of Oppression  30
Victory Arch Waterloo Railway Station  44
Violet Szabo and SOE Agents  45
Walthamstow War Memorial  16
Women of World War II  75
Wood Green War Memorial  38

# Websites used for reference

*https://historicengland.org.uk*
*www.britishlistedbuildings.co.uk*
*www.westminster-abbey.org*
*http://www.iwm.org.uk*
*http://bbm.org.uk*
*www.londonremembers.com*
*http://www.iwm.org.uk*
*https://www.guidelondon.org.uk*
*www.gov.uk*
*http://www.6millionmemorials.co.uk*
*www.secret-london.co.uk*
*https://c20society.org.uk*
*http://voiceseducation.org/content/katyn-massacre*
*http://stairwaytoheavenmemorial.org/*

www.ingramcontent.com/pod-product-compliance
Lightning Source LLC
Chambersburg PA
CBHW040735150426
42811CB00063B/1635